OXFORD MODERN LANGUAGES AND LITERATURE MONOGRAPHS

Editorial Committee

R. AUTY R. FARGHER C. GRAYSON
M. JACOBS A. J. KRAILSHEIMER A. W. RAITT
D. M. STEWART

THE WORD AND THE STONE

LANGUAGE AND IMAGERY IN NERUDA'S *CANTO GENERAL*

BY

FRANK RIESS

Pero una permanencia de piedra
y de palabra

OXFORD UNIVERSITY PRESS

1972

Oxford University Press, Ely House, London W. 1
GLASGOW NEW YORK TORONTO MELBOURNE WELLINGTON
CAPE TOWN IBADAN NAIROBI DAR ES SALAAM LUSAKA ADDIS ABABA
DELHI BOMBAY CALCUTTA MADRAS KARACHI LAHORE DACCA
KUALA LUMPUR SINGAPORE HONG KONG TOKYO

© OXFORD UNIVERSITY PRESS 1972

PRINTED IN GREAT BRITAIN
AT THE UNIVERSITY PRESS, OXFORD
BY VIVIAN RIDLER
PRINTER TO THE UNIVERSITY

TO MY WIFE
FRANCES

PREFACE

A STUDY of the *Canto general* is essential for an understanding of Neruda's poetry, and it is particularly important in view of the size of the work, which needs to be studied from many different angles. What follows is no more than an introduction to an enormous subject, and will, I hope, serve as a helpful basis for further study.

It is with pleasure that I express my gratitude to those who have helped me in preparing this book. I should like to thank Dr. C. A. Jones, whose advice through the whole period of research at Oxford was largely instrumental in getting it completed. Professor P. E. Russell and Dr. J. Franco were generous with their time and advice. I owe the greatest debt to Robert Pring-Mill, who encouraged me to clarify and develop my ideas on Neruda's poetry when I first began work on this study. He helped me to map out the subject and a critical approach to the *Canto general*.

I am also indebted to Professor L. Monguió of the University of California, Berkeley, who read the manuscript and offered valuable suggestions, to Sr. Neruda who graciously allowed me to quote so extensively from his work.

F. T. R.

Liverpool, 1971

CONTENTS

ABBREVIATIONS	xi
INTRODUCTION	xiii
The Sections of the *Canto general*	xviii
I. THE POET AND THE COLLECTIVITY	1
II. THE NATURAL PLANE OF REFERENCE	43
III. THE SOCIAL AND HISTORICAL PLANES OF REFERENCE	105
CONCLUSION	160
BIBLIOGRAPHY	165
INDEX	169

ABBREVIATIONS

P.N.	Pablo Neruda
L.S.	Claude Lévi-Strauss
B.H.S.	*Bulletin of Hispanic Studies*
C.A.	*Cuadernos americanos*
R.H.M.	*Revista hispánica moderna*
H.A.H.R.	*Hispanic-American Historical Review*
Y.A.J.	*Yale Architectural Journal*
F.C.E.	*Fondo de cultura económica*

INTRODUCTION

IN the *Canto general* Neruda examines themes which are common to many other Latin-American creative writers and artists; he shares an area of common purpose and values, and moves within a framework which is the same as that of Octavio Paz, Diego Rivera, Carlos Pellicer, and many other diverse personalities.

The similar preoccupations that these men share, the elaboration of a continuity with their historic and personal past, the attempts to define the authentic Latin-American man and his culture, these problems are far deeper than the surface political allegiances of these artists.[1] They are deeper because they consist in an emotional commitment to a way of life, even more particularly to a definition of life socially and morally. Nowadays, few writers and painters in Europe are engaged in such a task, the task of revealing a set of principles and a view of the world in terms of a structure of natural relationships which represents some kind of ideal or perfect order. Such tentative questions have an urgency about them, an existential quality that renders them very real to every Latin-American writer, because they confront him every day of his life when he looks around him. On the one hand he sees the richness, variety, and exuberance of the natural environment, and on the other — the poverty of the social order which is manmade; the latter is a pitiful complement to the former. If one is beautiful, fertile, varied, and perfect, the other is ugly, sterile, unrewarding, and exceedingly far from perfection. Theoretically, this is not new as a dilemma; but the important point is that it has an urgency that holds together much of the continent's writing and painting, in fact all forms of art.[2]

For this reason artistic and social creation are difficult to separate, and for this reason, too, writers come to be regarded as puppets of certain political ideologies. But to Pablo Neruda, and to many others, the perfection of their continent in terms of natural beauty and richness contrasts violently with the social ugliness and sterility

---

[1] J. Franco, *The Modern Culture of Latin America: Society and the Artist* (London, 1967), pp. 133–73.
[2] Ibid., pp. 265–6.

that has so far emerged. How, they ask, can the one come out of the other? If they possess such resources, such land, and such mountains, can they not have a comparable way of life that will in some measure reflect all this? Carlos Pellicer formulates this dilemma in a manner that echoes many other Latin-American poets:

> Hermosos y fuertes árboles!
> Como estos árboles han de ser un día
> en México, los hombres.[1]

Thus, politics in all its manifestations, the art of the possible, compromise, is but a shabby attempt to tinker with what is really a fundamental or almost religious dilemma. To be committed politically is only the tip of the iceberg, for beneath it hides a commitment that is much larger than any political label. It conceals a moral and philosophical determination to find and define a way of life, which will in some way complement, connect, and explain *hombre* in terms of his natural surroundings and generally his whole environment.[2]

Many critics have pointed to this fact with reference to the *Canto general*, but few have investigated the imagery of the poem in detail. The over-all framework of the poem impresses at first sight, and so do the many levels of reference contained in the one work. Rodríguez Monegal has commented: '... el Canto general es, a la vez y no sucesivamente, épico y lírico, crónica y autobiografía, dramatización histórica y dramatización personal.'[3] Other conclusions have repeatedly stressed this fact: the *Canto general* incorporates into one framework an astonishingly rich and varied range of experience and that the real achievement is the sheer organization of all this material into one vision of life. Ben Belitt considers that 'It ransacks the commonplace, the topical, the singular, in its search for the generic. The premise which it seems to have served is that imagination and the political factor, the meditative life and the existential datum, comprise a single reality.'[4] Finally, Luis Monguió has actually suggested that some kind of

[1] C. Pellicer, *Poema en tiempo vegetal, Material poético, 1918-1961* (Mexico, 1962), p. 413.
[2] J. Carrera Andrade, 'The New American and his point of view toward poetry', *Poetry*, vol. 62, No. 2 (May 1943), pp. 88–104.
[3] E. Rodríguez Monegal, *El viajero inmóvil* (Buenos Aires, 1966), p. 246.
[4] B. Belitt, Translator's Foreword to *Selected Poems of Pablo Neruda* (New York, 1961), p. 33.

world picture dominates the whole poem, and that the poet defines '. . . a Nerudian vision of the origin and creation of the world and American man'.[1]

To describe such a wide vision systematically is a very difficult task, but it could be achieved through an approach that attempted to view the *Canto general* as a whole, whilst examining particular contexts in some detail. This approach is what can be termed 'structuralism', for it brings together into one structure the content or themes of the *Canto general* with the organization of the imagery. Because of this, the images of the poem become signs of the poem's general frame of reference. More particularly, this study proposes to examine the imagery methodically and structurally on the various planes on which it operates. The analysis of the imagery will be as it refers outwards to various interconnected planes of reference emanating from the personal experience of the author himself. To achieve this, such an approach must unite levels of the poem into one structure, where historical events and personal experiences, cultural forms and natural forms, are integrated into one coherent vision. For it is this aspect, namely its integral quality, that makes the *Canto general* such an effective poem. Neruda has hinted as much recently in his definition of *patria*, where everything from the names of the plants to the spirit of the people is bound together into a living organic force.[2]

In certain respects the critical approach advocated here owes something to the writings of Claude Lévi-Strauss, but the extent of the debt should be clearly stated.[3] What is particularly advocated is his approach to the subject from certain aspects, and this does not imply an endorsement of his conclusions, nor does this book constitute an anthropological study. Because of the integral vision that the poet communicates in the *Canto general*, where all levels of experience are gathered together, it could be said that Neruda combines two approaches. First, he exhibits the emotional

[1] L. Monguió, Introduction to *Selected Poems of Pablo Neruda* (New York, 1961), p. 27. (B. Belitt has edited and translated the poems in this volume; Monguió has written the *Introduction*, pp. 7–29. Other articles by Belitt include 'Neruda and the gigantesque', *Poetry*, vol. 80, No. 2 (May 1952), pp. 116–18; 'The mourning Neruda', *Mundus Artium*, vol. 1, No. 1 (Winter 1967), pp. 14–23. This last article deals with poetry after the *Canto general*.)
[2] P.N., *Discursos* (with Nicanor Parra) (Santiago, 1962), p. 62.
[3] L.S., *The Savage Mind* (London, 1966); *Structural Anthropology* (New York, 1963); see also 'Les chats de Charles Baudelaire', *L'Homme* (Jan.–Apr. 1962), pp. 5–21.

feeling of a poet that in some manner the Latin-American man is the result of his natural environment, which shapes his concept of life and the world around him; and second, the poet feels the need to postulate in advance some totality, some integral vision or world picture. Just how these two are actually present and operate in the imagery of the poem is what this book seeks to examine.

The appreciation of a people's myths and rituals, and the logical equivalences that the mind constructs between natural and cultural patterns on various planes of meaning, play a crucial role in understanding and explaining the material conditions of existence of any people and their culture as a whole. Therefore these equivalences or relationships are functionally related to social organization and any other activity. It is these links and methods of analysis in Lévi-Strauss's writings that are of interest for the purpose of this work.

Finally, it should be noted what this study does not intend to examine. Because of the critical approach to the imagery, this inquiry will be dealing to a large extent with the content of the poem, but there will be no discussion or evaluation of the political or historical implications, or of the beliefs put across by Neruda about the history of his continent. Naturally, as they are most clearly communicated to the reader, they will have to be noted and described. But this will be in terms of recurring motifs or themes embodied in the major relationships of the *Canto general*'s imagery.

Neither will the *Canto general*'s structure be examined comparatively in relation to other examples of public and epic poetry. This could prove a very rich field of study; especially, for example, the epic formulas, static epithets, figurative tropes, and repeated paragraphs used by Neruda to address heroes or *libertadores*, could be profitably considered. Indeed, the formal structure of the poem and its main themes have yet to be adequately studied, especially in relation to other Chilean and Latin-American literary forms. Here, Neruda's stay in Mexico and his contact with a well-established social, historical, and literary tradition must have played an important part in shaping the *Canto general*.[1] A thorough

---

[1] Several writers in particular have commented on the relationship between the work of the Mexican muralists and the *Canto general*: e.g. A. Cardona Peña, *Pablo Neruda y otros ensayos* (Mexico, 1955), pp. 36–66; G. Bellini, *Introduzione a Neruda* (Milan, 1966), p. 23; A. Valbuena Briones, *Literatura hispanoamericana* (Barcelona, 1962), pp. 432–51; see also the author himself in 'Los frescos de Xavier Guerrero en Chillán', *Ars*, vol. 1, No. 5 (May 1943), pp. 60–2; 'Las vidas

examination of the literary background will probably show that the main themes of the *Canto general* as well as the imagery, however instinctive and emotional they may appear on the surface, can be seen in terms of formal codes and historical or literary conventions that constitute a common Latin-American tradition. Furthermore, Neruda's definition of man may prove to be considerably influenced by the apocalyptic and social vision of William Blake, a poet whom Neruda has translated. More study is needed to pinpoint the relationship that undoubtedly exists between Neruda and Quevedo, whose poetry Neruda has continually spoken of with profound understanding, and which is illuminating for an understanding of Neruda's attitude to death.[1]

In his 'Nerudian vision of the origin and creation of the world and American man' (Monguió, op. cit., p. 27) Neruda undoubtedly makes use of creation myths, golden-age myths, and many other archetypal formulas. This will also prove an interesting field of study, especially a comparison of his theory of the creation and origins of man with pre-Columbian beliefs. Here, it may be possible that the *Canto general* unites the modern consciousness with the mythic sensibility into one structure. More particularly it would be fruitful to examine the precise way that a historical or social event is compared to a mythical event, and hence the socio-historical level and the mythical level become intertwined.[2]

Except where otherwise stated, references to the works of Neruda are to the latest complete edition of his works, in two volumes (1968). In such references volume and page number alone will be given.[3]

del poeta', *O Cruzeiro Internacional* (Rio de Janeiro, 1 May 1962), pp. 32–5.

[1] P.N., '*Visions of the Daughters of Albion* and the *Mental Traveller* by William Blake', *Cruz y raya*, No. 20 (1934), pp. 85–109; 'Viaje al corazón de Quevedo', *Viajes* (Santiago, 1955), pp. 9–40; 'Cartas y sonetos de la muerte, de Quevedo', *Cruz y raya*, No. 33 (1935), pp. 83–101.

[2] See Mircea Eliade, *The Myth of the Eternal Return* (London, 1955) and *Myth and Reality* (London, 1964). These two works deal with the relationships between mythical forms and social forms, especially modern political ideology.

[3] P.N., *Obras completas*, tercera edición aumentada (2 vols., Losada, Buenos Aires, 1968), 1588+1649 pp.

The Sections of the *Canto general*

I. *La lámpara en la tierra*
II. *Alturas de Macchu-Picchu*
III. *Los conquistadores*
IV. *Los libertadores*
V. *La arena traicionada*
VI. *América, no invoco tu nombre en vano*
VII. *Canto general de Chile*
VIII. *La tierra se llama Juan*
IX. *Que despierte el leñador*
X. *El fugitivo*
XI. *Las flores de Punitaqui*
XII. *Los ríos del canto*
XIII. *Coral de año nuevo para la patria en tinieblas*
XIV. *El gran océano*
XV. *Yo soy*

I

THE POET AND THE COLLECTIVITY

TAKEN as a whole, the *Canto general* constitutes the definitive description of Pablo Neruda, both as a man, and in his relation to nature and to other men. These relationships can be discerned in the poem by drawing up various 'instrumental sets'. These are structures which link the poet as an individual to larger entities such as *pueblo* and *tierra*. Several self-contained sets can be enumerated which are the 'instrumental' ones, i.e. in the major structures which define the connections between man and nature, nature and the poet, at the most general level in the *Canto general*. The first requirement, therefore, would be to show how the poet as an individual becomes the spokesman of, and is identified with, the continent as a whole, through the essential equation *Hombre–Tierra*, and any others that may be found to exist.

The second requirement would be to point out how there arise from these instrumental sets smaller patterns which are a part of them, but which are used in various contexts of the poem, while they continually imply their general level of reference. Once a reader knows and understands these general, over-all instrumental sets, the *Canto general*'s precise field of reference becomes easier to examine. To take two examples: first—

> Aquí encontré el amor. Nació en la arena,
> creció sin voz, tocó los pedernales
> de la dureza y resistió a la muerte.
> Aquí el hombre era vida que juntaba
> la intacta luz, el mar sobreviviente,
> y atacaba y cantaba y combatía
> con la misma unidad de los metales.
>
> (i. 618)

What interests the poet here is the quality of group action, taken by men in a particular environment. The manner of these men is compared to the manner of metals, sea, and light. The lines imply a set and a system of relationships existing between man and nature. The second example will further illustrate this, and introduce another point in more detail:

> Patria, nave de nieve,
> follaje endurecido:
> allí naciste, cuando el hombre tuyo
> pidió a la tierra su estandarte
> y cuando tierra y aire y piedra y lluvia,
> hoja, raíz, perfume, aullido,
> cubrieron como un manto al hijo,
> lo amaron o lo defendieron.
> Así nació la patria unánime
> la unidad antes del combate.
>
> (i. 369)

Here the natural phenomena are taken to pieces and reconstructed into cultural concepts such as *patria*; the coming together of these is compared to the coming together of men, and when the two are put together there arises:

> ... la patria unánime
> la unidad antes del combate.[1]
>
> (i. 369)

What do these connections imply? Is there perhaps a set of general principles or relationships behind the *Canto general*, made up of the images used in differing contexts, which give it more form and unity than have hitherto been supposed? Do these relationships also stand for a coherent perspective of the poet himself and the world around him?

The opening sections of the *Canto general*, for example, state in great detail the nature and extent of the poet's relationship with other men and the world of matter and nature. The two sections *La lámpara en la tierra* (i. 319–34) and *Alturas de Macchu-Picchu* (i. 335–48) are both crucial to an understanding of the themes of the whole poem, working from the personal and private emotion of the poet as individual, to a general and integral vision of men

---

[1] A point of technique: Neruda's use of a *summation schema* shows the influence in his work of Spanish Golden Age poetry. For a history of the device see E. R. Curtius, *European Literature and the Latin Middle Ages* (New York, 1953), pp. 287–91; for a detailed discussion of it throughout Spanish literature see D. Alonso and C. Bousoño, *Seis calas en la expresión literaria española* (Madrid, 1963), p. 262; L. Spitzer mentions Neruda in *La enumeración caótica en la poesía moderna* (Buenos Aires, 1945), pp. 23 ff., 56 n., 68–72.

THE POET AND THE COLLECTIVITY

and the continent as a whole, of which the poet is a part.[1] In this chapter our first purpose is to catalogue these instrumental sets, and to observe how their presence is made manifest in any part of the poem, by the use of images that are from a part of one or another of the sets.

The first and most important instrumental set is the one which outlines and defines the connection that exists between *Hombre* and *Tierra*, a basic equation in the *Canto general*. The manner of equivalence of these two entities is the main source of connections and comparisons, and the intermediate parts of nature are the material itself of Neruda's vision. Beginning very simply, we could build the following set (Fig. 1). In this set the place of man in nature is defined as the climax of all the forms of nature. As man synthesizes all these, so equally does *Tierra*, the source of all life. This instrumental set is really the most general, because any part of nature can be fitted into it, and equally any reference in the poem can be worked back to it. Apart from placing man in some kind of scheme of creation, it works right through to the poet himself, who can then work outward on planes of increasing generality to the whole continent itself. The nature of the set is that one can refer both ways, i.e. *Hombre–Tierra*. Furthermore, the system can be isolated at any point, thus:

This, as we hope to show later on, is worked out very thoroughly throughout the *Canto general*.

The second instrumental set effects a comparison between *Hombre* and his parts and *Continente* and its parts. This is implied right at the beginning of the introductory poem:

---

[1] For a description of the discovery of this city, and a good set of photographs, see two books by H. Bingham, *Lost City of the Incas*, and *The Story of Machu Picchu and its Builders* (London, 1951). A more detailed architectural and archaeological survey, with many photographs, is *Machu Picchu, a Citadel of the Incas: Report of the Explorations and Excavations* (London, 1930). The conclusions about the dating of the site here are not generally held nowadays. A more recent survey is by G. Kubler, 'Machu Picchu', *Perspecta, Y.A.J.* vi (New Haven, Conn., 1960), pp. 48–55.

> Antes de la peluca y la casaca
> fueron los ríos, ríos arteriales:
>
> (i. 319)

Man as a sum of parts is merged into, and emerges out of, the continent, which is also a sum of parts coming together to form a unit (Fig. 2). This instrumental set connects with a related one, namely the comparison effected between America as a named continent and the female form. In *La lámpara en la tierra* (i. 319–334) and *Alturas de Macchu-Picchu* (i. 335–48) America is referred to by the following names:

> Útero verde, americana . . .
>
> (i. 322)
>
> Amada de los ríos, combatida
> por agua azul y gotas transparentes,
> como un árbol de venas es tu espectro . . .
>
> (i. 325)
>
> Madre de los metales, . . .
>
> (i. 327)
>
> Madre de las piedras . . .
>
> (i. 328)
>
> Antigua América, novia sumergida, . . .
>
> (i. 346)

The implications of this are better discussed when we come to consider the various planes of reference, but there can be no doubt that the fertility of the woman and the fertility of the soil are equated, especially since Neruda views past time in accumulated layers buried in the soil, and since later on the fertility of the soil serves to give a historical continuity to the recurring *libertadores* (i. 378–459). Moreover, the woman–earth equation serves to round off very neatly the notion that *Hombre* springs from the soil, and is made up of the earth itself.

When Neruda addresses the rivers of America (i. 325–7) he works geographically from north to south, just as he works from the head to the feet of the woman. A glance at the rivers shows this, where he moves down: Orinoco, Amazonas, Tequendama, Bío-Bío, the river of his own homeland. This parallels a similar movement when he describes the pre-Columbian peoples in *Los hombres* (i. 330–4): Tarahumara, Tarasco, Azteca, Maya, Inca, Araucano. Again, the last-named are the people with whom the poet feels most links, since he is one of their descendants. This movement describes the general framework, and the gradual and systematic movement down the continent to the particular place and tribe, which are (*a*) a part of the poet, and (*b*) a part of the continent as a whole, of which the poet is also a part. These dimensions of the poet's 'place' are important, and normally they are effectively combined, so that in practice it is difficult to separate these two levels, as the following extract shows:

> Pero háblame, Bío-Bío,
> son tus palabras en mi boca
> las que resbalan, tú me diste
> el lenguaje, el canto nocturno
> mezclado con lluvia y follaje.
>
> . . . . . .
>
> y luego te vi entregarte al mar
> dividido en bocas y senos,
> ancho y florido, murmurando
> una historia color de sangre.
>
> (i. 327)

The conscious mingling of the parts of the body and the parts of the continent is systematically carried out, and the intention of the poet is to 'place' himself as the recipient of the river itself. The body of the continent and the body of the poet become as if they were a single entity. Note, however, that through the parts of nature the poet always works through to man. The essential idea that these instrumental sets illustrate is the importance of man individually and collectively, both as a whole made up of parts, and as the most important entity in the poem. However varied and detailed the elements of nature, they exist in the scheme of the poem, as the example quoted shows, to illustrate man. These sets serve to outline the relationship of the poet with the continent and nature, since he is on the one hand a part of it, and on the other a microcosm of the whole. He is able by the connections outlined to become infinitely large or infinitely small, to identify himself systematically with anything and everything, to be a part and a whole, to be all men, or a man among many.[1] Such is the meaning of the final sentences in *Alturas de Macchu-Picchu*:

> Apegadme los cuerpos como imanes.
> Acudid a mis venas y a mi boca.
> Hablad por mis palabras y mi sangre.
>
> (i. 348)

---

[1] Monegal, op. cit., p. 246.

6 THE POET AND THE COLLECTIVITY

Here *por* is used in a double sense, meaning 'on behalf of', and 'through'. The poet has become a poet-spokesman and he does not speak himself, but others from the past and the present speak through him. The past yields up its forgotten words from the soil. The quotation illustrates now the relevance of the sets that have been discussed.

Another instrumental set that exists to define *Hombre* is the relationship between *hombre* and *océano*. In the section *El gran océano* (i. 654–92) the poet addresses the ocean as a whole, and also in its parts, especially in his classification of the creatures and plants that inhabit it. It is not the business of this chapter to examine in detail the meaning that *océano* embodies, but it is necessary to classify the elements or parts that Neruda uses when speaking of the whole body Ocean, since he uses them frequently to illustrate descriptions in different parts of the poem. The programme of *El gran océano* suggests that it might have been intended as a 'creation' piece for the *Canto general*, although it is very different from *La lámpara en la tierra*.[1] In this section of the *Canto general* a vast scheme of creation and natural phenomena is categorized. The programme of this section is not so cumulative as *La lámpara en la tierra*, but in *El gran océano* Neruda seems to have worked backwards in time from *hombre* to the sea, the stones, and the molluscs of the sea. The section ends with the birds of the coast (i. 687–9), *Phalacrocorax* and the albatross, and a final evocation of the sea as a whole *La noche marina* (i. 690–2), where the dominant image is again the female form, which appears in great detail and is very particularly described.

Taking the equation *Hombre–Océano* (see Fig. 3) the same process of isolation can be put into effect, which parallels the one described on page 4:

[1] Nevertheless, the section has affinities with *La lámpara en la tierra*:
Todo era ser, substancia temblorosa,
pétalos carniceros que mordían,
acumulada cantidad desnuda,
palpitación de plantas seminales, ...   (i. 657)
Compare with *Vegetaciones* (i. 320–2) in *La lámpara en la tierra*.

THE POET AND THE COLLECTIVITY

Further on it will be possible to show not only how each of these breaks down into further subdivisions, but how in many cases the separate *Océano* and *Tierra* sets are merged into one overall cosmology.

A further instrumental set would be that which describes the ocean in terms of a woman (see Fig. 4). This is particularly evident in the final poem of *El gran océano* entitled *La noche marina* (i. 690–2), which forms a résumé of the section as a whole. The poet reiterates a desire to become merged as a whole with the whole of the sea:

> Quiero tener tu frente simultánea,
> abrirla en mi interior para nacer
> en todas tus orillas, ir ahora
> con todos los secretos respirados,
> con tus oscuras líneas resguardadas
> en mí como la sangre o las banderas,
> llevando estas secretas proporciones
> al mar de cada día, a los combates
> que en cada puerta — amores y amenazas —
> viven dormidos. (i. 691)

These constitute the sum total of the instrumental sets in the *Canto general*; but they are so general that every plant, creature, or mineral can be fitted into them. It remains now to show how the poet operates within this over-all framework, how he implies reference to these in any particular part of the poem, and how, as we move into particular focus, the technique becomes increasingly complex. This can be said to be analogous to languages whose basic structures are relatively simple, but difficult to arrive at. The multiplicity of elements and their combinations obscure the clear and simple general structures.[1] In any case general frameworks of reference, or instrumental sets as they are called here, are so large that they could invite criticism for the following reasons: (*a*) they must be related to the specific working of the poem; and (*b*) they do not 'structure' the elements inside them sufficiently; or, to put it in another manner, they are not committed to any particular explanation. Only when it can be shown how they are contained in particular and specific instances in the poem will they acquire any meaning or validity.

The instrumental sets outlined so far bring together the shape

---

[1] L.S., 'Linguistics and anthropology', in *Structural Anthropology*, p. 68.

of man and the shape of natural forms. In the *Canto general* the poet observes in the forms that nature takes a device for comparing the form that man and society take. Furthermore, the substance of matter in nature itself is compared and seen as a part of the essence of man himself. This last statement should be evident if the two main instrumental sets outlined are observed. They show *Océano* and *Tierra* at the other end of an equation with *Hombre*. Between these two poles all the objects of nature, both in form and substance, are fed into *Hombre* or *Océano/Tierra* (see Figs. 1, 3). The movement can be taken both ways. In the initial poem of the *Canto general* (i. 319-20) man made up of mud is paralleled by objects formed of earth and substances of the earth, so that a double equation ensues:

A. Objects made up of elements of the earth;
B. Man made up of elements of the earth.

Both A and B comprise definite forms: *hombre, vasija, forma de la arcilla, copa imperial*. Man is a unity, therefore, a 'whole' or self-contained system made up of parts (Figs. 5, 6). Nature, too, is populated with animal, vegetable, and mineral forms which can be viewed as 'wholes', but also as parts of the 'whole' of man. From the instrumental sets that have so far been classified the shape of man and the shape of the sea and continent can be carefully compared. In this case, it should be noted that a man (as a member of a species) has to be viewed quite apart from any biological connotations, in a double sense. It is a question of considering his organism as a self-contained system, and his membership of a species which is in turn a system, i.e. *pueblo*. Man's form then is a conceptual tool, so to speak, which can be referred to as a whole or in parts, and in this manner compared to other 'wholes' and 'parts' on related planes of reference. This is equally applicable to any other parts of the instrumental set, such as *árbol* or *ola*. In this respect the following cluster of concepts are extremely important in the *Canto general: estatua, forma, sistema, organización, unidad, extensión*, and such verbs as *construir, elevar, organizar*, where the action brought about by the joining up of people to form units such as *pueblo* and *patria* is paralleled or compared with the organization and structure of *árbol* or *ola*. To take an example, the opening poem of *Los libertadores* (i. 378-80) has an immense theme on several planes, which is clearly defined by the shape and parts

THE POET AND THE COLLECTIVITY 9

of the tree. The constant renewal of the tree, through the roots in the soil, on a natural plane is parallel to the continuity of *libertadores* on a historical plane, whose bodies feed the blood of the continent (see Fig. 2); and it also gives rise to organized resistance in the shape of people coming together to form *pueblo*:

> Asómate a su cabellera:
> toca sus rayos renovados:
> hunde la mano en las usinas
> donde su fruto palpitante
> propaga su luz cada día.
> (i. 379)

The identification of the poet with people, and people as a whole with *árbol*, is incomprehensible without having the *Hombre–Tierra* (Fig. 1) equation clearly defined. Here, the poet isolates one branch of the instrumental set:

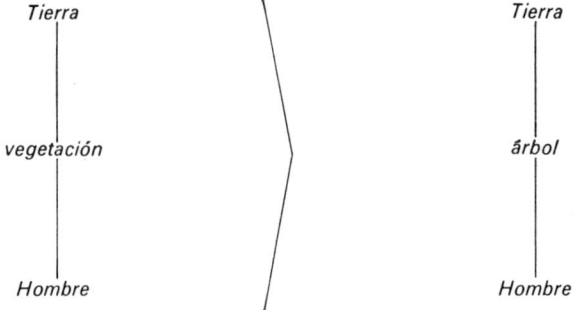

As *pueblo* signifies unity, organization, and a positive system, so, in this particular case, does the tree:

> Aquí viene el árbol, el árbol
> cuyas raíces están vivas,
> sacó salitre del martirio,
> sus raíces comieron sangre
> y extrajo lágrimas del suelo:
> las elevó por sus ramajes,
> las repartió en su arquitectura.
> (i. 378)

The men that emerge from the earth organize themselves in the same way as the growth of the tree, and take on the shape and architecture of *árbol*. In this context the tree is the largest image that refers outwards, but it involves the instrumental set *Hombre–Tierra* (see Fig. 1). The poet uses the tree as a conceptual device to define the limits of the poem's field of reference:

> ... monta guardia en la frontera,
> en el límite de sus hojas.
>
> (i. 380)

The tree has several meanings in the one poem, as for instance when it illustrates some important historical and social themes which are constantly occurring in the *Canto general*, and which will be examined separately elsewhere. Another important example of the isolation of one part of an instrumental set is the following, taken from *Hombre–Océano* (Fig. 3):

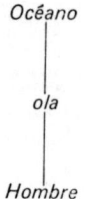

Looking at *ola*, the poet is seen to break it down to:

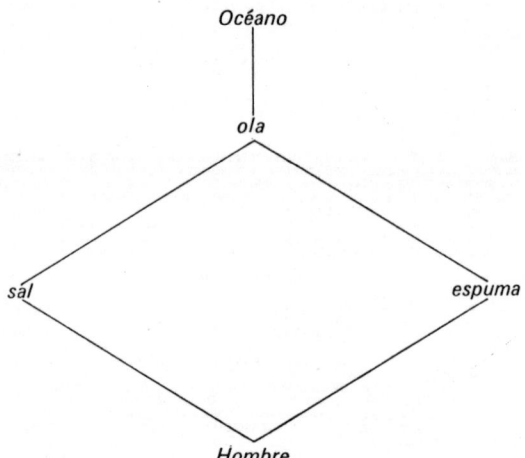

These aspects of a wave are the ones that are constantly selected for *ola*; moreover, either *sal* or *espuma* can be taken sometimes to

THE POET AND THE COLLECTIVITY 11

imply the parts or elements of the set, and refer back to *océano* as a whole. *Ola* embodies all the visible and endless energy of the sea, which is bringer of both life and death. *Ola*, therefore, has retained the essential characteristics of the sea:

> . . . .
> el mar cayó como una gota ardiendo
> de distancia en distancia, de hora en hora:
> su fuego azul se convirtió en esfera,
> el aire de sus ruedas fue campana,
> su interior esencial tembló en la espuma,
> y en la luz de la sal fue levantada
> la flor de su espaciosa autonomía.
> (i. 656)

The particular shape that the *espaciosa autonomía* takes is compared to *flor*, here used in the same sense as *árbol* to express the form and organization of the sea as an independent 'whole'. When Neruda has occasion to address *ola* directly, he uses the same set of associations:

> La escuela de la sal abrió las puertas,
> voló toda la luz golpeando el cielo,
> creció desde la noche hasta la aurora
> la levadura del metal mojado,
> toda la claridad se hizo *corola*,
> creció *la flor* hasta gastar la piedra, . . .
> (i. 670)

The movement of the wave crashing on the rocks is a fragment of *océano* as a whole delivering a measure of its total energy, force, and unity, and the movement is arrested in the substance of *espuma* and *sal*, the shape and organization of the wave, in the shape and organization of a flower. The ambiguous role of the wave and its function as a part of the whole of the sea are stated in this manner:

> . . . .
> es la unidad del mar que se construye:
> la columna del mar que se levanta:
> todos sus nacimientos y derrotas.
> (i. 670)

This illustration is included to clarify observations about the instrumental sets, rather than to explain the meaning of the ocean in Neruda's cosmology; but it can be usefully taken as an introduction to later remarks.

Sal and *espuma* are sometimes used on their own and in connection with other instrumental sets whilst implying their original frames of reference. For example, in an otherwise obscure section, knowledge of the instrumental sets makes the following reference clearer:

> Madre de piedra, espuma de los cóndores.
>
> (i. 339)

Where the shape of a wave over the sea is like a range of mountains over land, the positions of *nieve* and *espuma* by association become interchangeable. Hence the high situation of the city of Machu-Picchu in the peaks of the *cordillera* is likened to the tip of the waves. Furthermore, the *cóndor* is a bird of prey that flies very high, a fact that is particularly important in Neruda's cosmology.

> y sobre las plumas carnívoras
> volaba encima del mundo
> el cóndor . . .
> talismán negro de la nieve, . . .
>
> (i. 324)

Taking the connections still further, in the opening lines of the *Canto general*, the *cordillera* is described as the shape of the waves:

> . . . .
> fueron las cordilleras, en cuya onda raída
> el cóndor o la nieve parecían inmóviles:
>
> (i. 319)

Here *cóndor* is again associated with 'wave' through its original connection with mountain peaks and snow; the circle is closed if we come back to the poem *La ola* (i. 670), where a description of the wave finishes with the following comparison:

> hasta que de las ramas en la fuerza
> despegó su nevado poderío.
>
> (i. 670)

These connections matter, for they enable the poet to choose within a definable framework and to make comparisons which may

THE POET AND THE COLLECTIVITY

appear as random ones, but which betray a coherent set of general principles.[1]

If any of these elements (see Fig. 7) can be associated, it becomes of some importance to clarify the instrumental set, in order to comprehend the meaning fully in a particular case. A passage from *Alturas de Macchu-Picchu* brings into relief the process under discussion:

> Pero una permanencia de piedra y de palabra:
> la ciudad como un vaso se levantó en las manos
> de todos, vivos, muertos, callados, sostenidos
> de tanta muerte, un muro, de tanta vida un golpe
> de pétalos de piedra: la rosa permanente, la morada: 5
> este arrecife andino de colonias glaciales.
> Cuando la mano de color de arcilla
> se convirtió en arcilla, y cuando los pequeños
>   párpados se cerraron
> llenos de ásperos muros, poblados de castillos,
> y cuando todo el hombre se enredó en su agujero, 10
> quedó la exactitud enarbolada:
> el alto sitio de la aurora humana:
> la más alta vasija que contuvo el silencio:
> una vida de piedra después de tantas vidas.
>
> (i. 341)

These lines illustrate the point that the instrumental sets bring together the shape and substance of man and those of nature or man-made objects. In this extract there is a contrast between the life of men and the life of the city, a continual movement between the form and substance of the city and the form and substance of man. The final line shows how so many lives become one in the shape of the stone that makes up the essential matter of the city. The city of Machu-Picchu[2] as a whole synthesizes all the different strands of Neruda's cosmology, as for example the address to the city in Section IX (i. 343-4) clearly demonstrates. There, all the forms and substances of the instrumental sets come together; stone,

---

[1] The wave is compared to the mountain peaks through *espuma* and *nieve*; also to a *rosa*, because of its organization and flowerings, and finally to *árbol* through *ramas de la fuerza*. These connections will be discussed further on.

[2] The usual spelling of this name is different from the one that Neruda uses in the title of the poem. For this reason, when referring to the city by name the correc tspelling is retained: Machu-Picchu not Macchu-Picchu. This is an error that has become accepted in the text of the poem since the first edition of 1946.

metal, earth, sea, beasts, and birds (both as species and particular named ones). Especially emphasized is the position of the city, and this fact illustrates the point made earlier in connection with the relationship between *cordillera/ola* (see Fig. 7).

> Cordillera esencial, techo marino.
> Arquitectura de águilas perdidas.
> (i. 344)

Here, the city's position and construction are brought out. It is the city as a unit, and the city as a single pattern of interconnected shapes (*arquitectura*), that seize the poet's imagination. Through these two concepts the poet arrives at a definition of man both as a unit or whole in himself and as a part of a larger whole; this is just like the city, which is made up of autonomous stones which come together to form a single construction. The stone of the city is the crucial element isolated from *Hombre* ⇌ *Tierra*, but the movement between man and matter is expressed conceptually through the shape of *vaso*, which enables the poet to abstract logically and connect both the city and man as shapes or quantities that are linked. The unity and organization of the city are compared to the organization and unity of the *vaso*.

The movement from lines 1 to 6 is:

> permanencia de piedra y de palabra:
> ciudad como un vaso . . .
> muro, . . .
> pétalos de piedra: . . .
> rosa permanente . . .
> arrecife . . .

Both the 'wholeness' and the permanence strike the poet, but it is a permanence attributable only to man who formed it, so the movement cannot end there. The death of man is seen as part of the existence of stone itself, which also makes the different deaths of the builders into one collective death, just as they made the different stones into one unity or whole; i.e. the city with its *arquitectura*.[1] The death of the builders is seen as part of the existence of the stone itself, its very exactitude and perfection is the

[1] See R. Pring-Mill, Introduction to *The Heights of Macchu Picchu*, trans. N. Tarn (London, 1966), p. 12.

THE POET AND THE COLLECTIVITY

exactitude and perfection of men as both separate individual units and collective units shaping the stone into an outline whose organization and beauty has a form and an essence parallel to those of natural forms. Thus there is a movement from the form of man to man-made forms to natural forms.

Vaso is a form which not only indicates a shape made by man, but is itself a comparison with man (see Figs. 5, 6). Therefore we have *hombre, vaso, ciudad* all connected through form and substance; and this relationship implies or leads through to the *Hombre* ⇌ *Tierra* instrumental set. Note how the collective death becomes transformed into an image that survives, i.e. *vaso* (see line 2), which refers to the city or the collectivity that built the city. The whole city is perched upon mountain peaks (line 2), which are like the human fingers of the continent, or the waves of the sea. In both cases it rises above the surface of the earth and sea (see 'Madre de piedra, espuma de los cóndores' (i. 339)), so that it does not lose its shape and identity by becoming submerged. In line 4 the *muro*, whose organization and perfection are like a flower that endures in the constant cycle of nature, is made up of stones whose function as parts of the wall is likened to the petals of a rose as parts of a flower.[1] It is also, of course, the walls of *vaso*, which, like the whole of the city, can be broken up into parts for the city to be examined in parts. But above all, this line and the following emphasize how the concept of the life and the death of the builders has been discerned or caught in the substance and the shape of the stone, thus:

> . . . . . .
> la ciudad como un vaso se levantó en las manos
> de todos, vivos, muertos, callados, sostenidos
> de tanta muerte, un muro, de tanta vida un golpe
> de pétalos de piedra: la rosa permanente, . . .
>
> (i. 341)

The death of all is as present as the wall, and yet its permanence and life are like a rose which never died. Here, *golpe* can mean either the work and energy involved in the building of the wall, or more particularly the *golpe* or crowd of people, here referring to the anonymous mass that built the wall, i.e. *pueblo*. Neruda uses the

---
[1] R. Pring-Mill, op. cit., p. 12.

rose here as a conceptual device to bring across the idea of life, organization, and beauty.¹

Finally, the city as a reef rising above the sea, *arrecife* (line 6), continues the idea of stones or rocks as matter that endures the constant action of the waves, which, like time, are constantly eroding the natural forms. This comparison is permissible if earlier remarks are cogent.²

The position of the city is a quality which explains its permanence: it is above the waves which would bury it. More important for our purpose, however, is the fact that it implies the instrumental sets in the background and explains apparently emotional or illogical juxtapositions. Lines 7–14 take one through from the life of man himself to his death and existence in the substance and shape of the stone. Neruda works from the parts of man in lines 7 and 8 to *todo el hombre* in line 10. This movement is a development of lines 1–6, since now man is described as *vaso* and, by implication, as the city as well. Man returns in his death to his original substances, into the shape and substance of *vaso*: so, n line 10,

. . . .
y cuando todo el hombre se enredó en su agujero, . . .

the *vaso*, *hombre*, *ciudad* network linked by form and substance is abstracted successively, and what remains is a substance and a shape which embodies the collective whole of man, and man as an individual. Thus the movement of the images develops in the following manner where the city begins to lead through to the

---

¹ See *Oda al edificio*:
>El hombre
>separará la luz de las tinieblas
>y así
>como venció su orgullo vano
>e implantó su sistema
>para que se elevara el edificio,
>seguirá construyendo
>la rosa colectiva,
>reunirá en la tierra
>el material huraño de la dicha
>y con razón y acero
>irá creciendo
>el edificio de todos los hombres.
>   (i. 1049)

² Madre de piedra, espuma de los cóndores.
Alto arrecife de la aurora humana.
                                    (i. 339)

growth and dawn of a new life which was buried but potentially obtainable all the time:

>   exactitud enarbolada . . .   11
>   alto sitio de la aurora humana . . .   12
>   la más alta vasija que contuvo el silencio . . .   13
>   una vida de piedra después de tantas vidas.   14

Here the position of the city, and the city as a shape which implies man and life, both similar to man and a part of him (*vasija*), lead the poet through to the man himself, who is an entity apart from all these substances, i.e. *piedra arcilla*, but linked in his origins to them (see Fig. 8). The men of Machu-Picchu are dead, but their death has assumed a shape and a meaning which will live on in the present. This is evident if we look at the last line,

>   . . . .
>   una vida de piedra después de tantas vidas.

The function of this commentary is to bring into relief the technique which operates in the *Canto general*, and which in every case implies the instrumental sets that define and describe *hombre* in the most general terms. The movement in the above piece is the same in Section XI of *Alturas de Macchu-Picchu* (i. 346–7), where the measure and proportion of the stone are related to the activity of *hombre*. Nor is it a question of the stone's disappearing; the movement of the poetry shows that there exists a coherent set of general relationships logically centred upon *hombre*, which enables the poet to move within and about natural forms and substances, so that he can build cultural concepts such as *patria* and *pueblo*. Hence the remarks earlier, about the anatomical shape of man and his parts relate here to the shape and parts of the city. But this same man is a member of a collectivity or species, so that the collectivity can be defined equally by the shape and parts of the city, of man, and of *vaso*. Nor is the process limited just to *hombre*; the exactitude of the city perched on the mountain peaks is compared to the shape and outline of a tree (line 11), and the penultimate line has the same *vaso* image as line 2:

>   . . . .
>   la más alta vasija que contuvo el silencio: . . .

The approach from particular context to general frames of

reference in this piece shows how the main image of *vaso* brings together both *hombre* and *Macchu-Picchu*, in its substance and form. Nor is it merely the stone of the *vaso*; a further possibility is the clay of *vaso* and *hombre*, as shown in lines 7 and 8. This reinforces the notion of *vaso* as a substance and a form which indicates man: man has already been referred to as *forma de la arcilla* in the preceding section of the *Canto general* (i. 319). This, however, illustrates the role the instrumental sets play in any particular context of the poem—the pieces being taken out and recast in the heat of the poem, but their original reference back to the general scheme remaining unchanged. The parts can be rearranged according to what axis of reference one cares to adopt; so that the various networks of comparison in this passage are:

(A) A comparison between the parts of the city and the parts of man, leading to a comparison between the city and man as a unified whole.
(B) A tracing backwards to the common substance of *hombre*, *ciudad*, and *vaso* in *Tierra*, through *piedra* and also *arcilla*, which links *hombre*, *vaso*, and *Tierra*.
(C) A comparison between the form of the city and the form of man, and the shape that their collective effort embodies in the work they poured into the shaping of the city.
(See Fig. 8).

The various groups and patterns of relationships that can be discerned always relate back to the major relationship of the instrumental sets.

A similar organization could be deduced from any part of the *Canto general*, where the movement of the poetry links the various elements of any instrumental set through to the shape and substance of man and to that of matter. Why is this possible? Because the poet has in the background the sets that connect man up with *Tierra* and *Océano* (Figs. 1, 3), and these two subdivide into the forms that inhabit both these different natural domains. Furthermore, by connecting these wholes up to *hombre*, it is possible to consider any concept, however large, in terms of the human scale. The poetry of the *Canto general* is, therefore, an attempt to classify and systematize the human form, not out of any erotic curiosity, but by the idea that all proportions and harmony begin there.

Another poem, *Los constructores de estatuas (Rapa Nui)* from *El gran océano* (i. 661–3), illustrates the last point. The poem is about the men who built the statues on Easter Island; it is also a comparison between the men who built them and the statues themselves, a comparison which links the survival of man and the survival of the statue, the origins of man and the origins of the statue, and the substance and form of both. The movement is much the same as in the previous extract, for the statue remains, but the substance and shape of man are contained in it as well.

. . . .
La estatua que creció sobre nuestra estatura.
(i. 662)

Here, too, the shape moves outward to confront the shape of the sea, itself referred to as *estatua* in the final poem in the section *La noche marina* (i. 690). The movement of time shapes matter just as the waves do the rocks of the coast, but the shape of the stone carved by man remains and retains the life and activity of the man who formed it.

> Miradlas hoy, tocad esta materia, estos labios
> tienen el mismo idioma silencioso que duerme
> en nuestra muerte, y esta cicatriz arenosa,
> que el mar y el tiempo como lobos han lamido,
> eran parte de un rostro que no fue derribado,
> punto de un ser, racimo que derrotó cenizas.
> (i. 662–3)

The shape and substance of man can be discerned and touched on the worn-out surface of the stone which bears the marks of his work on it. The connection between matter and man in relation to the poet who discerns it is seen as *idioma silencioso*. What does *idioma* mean in this context? How does it refer outwards?

In the *Canto general* there are the following images for language:

> idioma —— palabra, sílaba.
> alfabeto —— letras, iniciales.

The concept of *idioma* is a device in the poem that enables the poet to organize and build unities such as *pueblo* and *patria*; it enables him to refer to parts and wholes in the manner outlined. This scheme is also used throughout the *Canto general* to illustrate the kind of language which is revealed to the poet, and also to show how any particular object comes across as a structural whole, i.e. as *idioma* which is meaningful and intelligible to the poet. Describing the *hombre* in the opening lines of the *Canto general*,

> ... en la empuñadura
> de su arma de cristal humedecida,
> las *iniciales de la tierra* estaban
> escritas. (i. 319)

This set of images pertaining to *alfabeto* establishes a connection between the shapes and substances of the earth and sea and the cultural forms of man, which leads to the language of *hombre* and finishes with the words of the poet himself. By means of linking *hombre* to *Tierra* and *Océano* the poet has another conceptual device which enables him to identify himself with the continent itself and the collective aspect of *pueblo*:

> Tierra mía sin nombre, sin América,
> . . . .
> tu aroma me trepó por las raíces
> hasta la copa que bebía, hasta la más delgada
> palabra aún no nacida de mi boca.
> (i. 320)

The impression is of a movement from *Tierra* to *raíces* to *cuerpo* and finally to *boca*;[1] and *palabra* links up with *iniciales de la tierra* earlier in the same poem (i. 319). In the description of the city of Machu-Picchu the poet concentrates on linking the form of the city to the men who built it; consequently one of the crucial images is that of language, which survives to tell of other men's achievements to the poet, who then communicates this to us through the medium of the poem:

> Pero una permanencia de piedra y de palabra: ...
> (i. 341)

This permanence, which survives, contrasts with the disappearance of the fragments of the everyday life of the inhabitants of the city.

---

[1] A similar movement occurs in i. 327:
> y luego te vi entregarte al mar
> dividido en bocas y senos,
> ancho y florido, murmurando
> una historia color de sangre.

> ... porque todo, ropaje, piel, vasijas,
> palabras, vino, panes,
> se fue, cayó a la tierra.
>
> (i. 340)

This is repeated again in the following section:

> . . . .
> cuanto fuisteis cayó: costumbres, sílabas
> raídas, máscaras de luz deslumbradora.
>
> (i. 341)

Later on the movement of the poem begins to emphasize the coming together of these parts (*sílabas, palabras*) to form a recognizable pattern with meaning for the poet. In Section VIII (i. 341–3) there are the following examples:

> Sube conmigo, amor americano.
> . . . . . .
> Oh, Wilkamayu de sonoros hilos,
> . . . . . .
> qué *idioma* traes a la oreja apenas
> desarraigada de tu espuma andina?
> . . . . . .
> Qué dicen tus destellos acosados?
> Tu secreto relámpago rebelde
> antes viajó poblado de *palabras*?
> Quién va rompiendo *sílabas* heladas
> *idiomas* negros, estandartes de oro,
> *bocas* profundas, *gritos* sometidos,
> en tus delgadas aguas arteriales?

The poet and his subject are moving closer together as he asks the river, the mountains, and the city to yield up their meaning, their past, the men who lived and died amongst these forms. Questions about the origin of the river should be viewed as questions related to *hombre*, as the last lines quoted demonstrate.

This language is the *idioma* whose pattern and meaning the poet is trying to discern. It is the story of the men of the city, which is revealed to him in the shape and substance of natural forms or those which have been made by man himself. The *idioma* is conclusively established when the poet's vision of man and his environment comes together as a meaningful pattern which can be compared to the meaningful pattern of language. Hence:

22 THE POET AND THE COLLECTIVITY

> Yo vengo a hablar por vuestra boca muerta.
>
> . . . .
>
> contadme todo, cadena a cadena,
>
> . . . .
>
> Acudid a mis venas y a mi boca.
> Hablad por mis palabras y mi sangre.
>
> (i. 347–8)

The whole of the *Canto general* is a story whose language the poet discerns, but which others speak for him. Language as an organized form is parallel to organized forms such as *piedra*, *metal*, which in turn are parts of a larger organization. Thus to return to the Easter Island statues:

> Miradlas hoy, tocad esta materia, estos labios
> tienen el mismo idioma silencioso que duerme
> en nuestra muerte, . . .
>
> (i. 662–3)

What can be said of the use of *idioma* in this context is analogous to our points made earlier about the form and substance of matter. For here the poet is touching the statue of stone shaped by a man many centuries ago, and through the shape of the statue he arrives at the shape of the man; the process is similar if one thinks of the substance of the stone leading through to the substance of man. The overriding idea that is communicated, then, is that the death of the stone-carver has not been lost: of course he is dead, but his death has assumed a substance and a shape in the statue. This is exactly what the reference to *idioma* accomplishes. As a medium of communication it brings across to the poet the death of the man who carved the statue, and incorporates it into the meaning of our own existence. But it comes out of the stone statue, which is a unified structure like *idioma*. Therefore the parts of *idioma* are used as signs which imply and lead the poet to a larger over-all meaning, as the extracts from *Alturas de Macchu-Picchu* (i. 335–48) show. *Idioma* is thus used metaphorically, with the effect that the image as a whole works by establishing a significant link between two fields of association. The above examples should show that it serves to reinforce the connection of *Hombre* to *Tierra* and *Océano* (see Figs. 1, 3), by using the parts of the instrumental sets and establishing a comparison between these and the organization of language as a whole made up of parts which have meaning for the

THE POET AND THE COLLECTIVITY 23

author. This should lead through to the other use of *idioma* in the *Canto general*; namely that it is a language with a meaning as well as a structure. *Idioma* can refer to the language of meaning that is communicated to the author, as well as to a structural comparison between parts and wholes.

The following examination of *A pesar de la ira* from *Los conquistadores* (i. 376–7) should lead the argument from a consideration of the above question through to a more detailed examination of the particular role of specific names and numbers in a language of reference, as well as a consideration of its organizational nature. We are trying here, in other words, to show the capacity that the images have to refer from the most general properties and elements of a system down to the individual name of a tree or a historical figure. But first we must examine how the relationships of *Hombre* ⇌*Tierra* are set up.

> Roídos yelmos, herraduras muertas!
> Pero a través del fuego y la herradura
> como de un manantial iluminado
> por la sangre sombría,
> con el metal hundido en el tormento   5
> se derramó una luz sobre la tierra:
> número, nombre, línea y estructura.
> Páginas de agua, claro poderío
> de idiomas rumorosos, dulces gotas
> elaboradas como los racimos,   10
> sílabas de platino en la ternura
> de unos aljofarados pechos puros,
> y una clásica boca de diamantes
> dio su fulgor nevado al territorio.
>
>   (i. 376–7)

In this passage the positive aspects of the Spanish Conquest are integrated into the relationship between *Hombre* and *Tierra/Océano*, and as history progresses the *conquista* becomes part of the enduring or structural order which persists beneath the order of events; it is itself a transient, changing, and conflicting order. By the poet's definition of *hombre* in relation to *Tierra* and *Océano*, the Spanish conquest is subsumed into a larger frame of reference. 'A través del fuego y la herradura' recalls a similar movement in *Alturas de Macchu-Picchu* 'A través del confuso esplendor' (i. 346). This line is not unconnected, since it initiates the same movement of getting behind external shapes and structures into the internal or reconstituted ones. Whereas in *Alturas de Macchu-Picchu* the line and proportion of the stone were a pleasure and a perfection in themselves, which had to be reassessed into a new relationship with *hombre*, here the externals of the *conquista* are violent and conflicting, and the whole pattern of relationships which is born out of it is difficult to discern. This passage shows, for example, how printing as communication, and the Spanish language as a unifying force, give rise to a unity expressed by the people and nations that will arise after the bloodshed and conflict have subsided. The emergence and growth of this structure are like the bubbling of water, the spreading of light, or the unfolding of a plant or a tree, which derive their nourishment from the soil; and like the image of the tree it opens out to reveal its autonomous organization and structure. The image of the tree in line 10 will be taken up in much greater detail in the following section of the poem, *Los libertadores* (i. 378–459). Its growth in the final lines of *Los conquistadores* foreshadows the next section, which opens with *árbol*.

The death and the passing away of the *conquista* is evoked by the debris of objects which will be eaten away by time, but which can also lead through to a reconstituted *hombre* and his connection with *Tierra/Océano*. These objects (*yelmo, herradura*) betray the hand of man; they are shaped by man and made up of metal which is incorporated in the minerals of the earth. They imply and lead us through to the structural order beneath or behind the insignificant pile of the surface events. The re-emerging structure is like a light that spreads over the earth; this has come out of the blood and the torment of the *conquista* (lines 3–5). This parallels the movement of the blood of the dead spilled into the soil, and the objects of line 1, as *metal hundido*. This becomes the water of the *manantial* spreading light over the earth. The association between water and blood recalls earlier suggestions made of *Río–Agua— Arterias–Sangre* (see Fig. 2), where the parts of the body and its elements become identified and intermingled with the parts and the elements of *Tierra* (i. 326–7). But here these elements, *sangre*, *metal*, became reconstituted out of the soil into *luz*, and more specifically into the attributes of line 7, which are particularly important. For the poet, therefore, the organization and form, the name and the number of any structure are describable. Furthermore, it is crucial for him to use these attributes, so that he can work through to the same qualities in both social and man-made forms. There has been a movement in this poem from order of events to a structural order, from disorder to order, from death to life. The importance of the concepts in line 7 cannot be overemphasized, for these are mediators between the shape and parts of man and the shape and parts of nature. In other words, the poet is able to compare the proportions of any and every object to those of man, and such cultural forms as *pueblo*, by using *número*, *nombre*, *línea*, *estructura*.

Lines 8–14 take up *luz sobre la tierra* in more detail, leading us through to a comparable image, but now much more specific and clearly defined than in line 6:

> ... dio su fulgor nevado al territorio.

Thus, where we had *luz* and *tierra* in line 6, in the final line the poet has a comparable but more particular *fulgor*, *nevado*, and *territorio*, which refers to a more specific region that derives from the general *luz* and *tierra*. What has occurred? The process in between has shown in more detail the parts that go to make up line 6 and rendered them more particular and specific. Lines 8–14 show how the structure that unfolds is compared in *número*, *nombre*, *línea*, and *estructura* to the attributes of man and a language. Lines 6 and 7 describe the essential substance and shape of this light, lines 8–14 give it a more particular delineation.

The movement of water and the movement of language and learning are resolved in line 8, where the spring of water which is described as coming out of the soil, out of the blood and torment of the *conquista*, communicates a social as well as a natural sound, i.e. the sound of water and language, whose organization and beneficial effects are likened to the autonomous structure and architecture of the branches in a tree (*racimo*). This language, before only spoken, and now written, is made up of the parts that come out of the soil: hence *manantial* gives forth water composed of drops, compared in its form and organization to syllables and language. The organization and structure of language are linked to the natural organization and structure of *agua*, and ultimately *Tierra* (see Fig. 9), from whence it springs. The importance of the concepts in line 7 brings us to a central problem in the poetry of the *Canto general*. Much has been said up till now about the comparisons effected between the form and the substance of nature and man. The relationships can be mapped out in the instrumental sets, as is evident in the words *línea* and *estructura*; but what about *número* and *nombre*? Can these in any way be seen as the names and numbers of people and other natural forms which imply at a more general level their *línea* and *estructura*?

For the poet, the importance of number and name and line and structure is that they enable him to classify and categorize the endless variety of nature, but also they permit him to discern the origins and the substance of man himself in particular named or classified forms and their own autonomous organization (see Fig. 8c). The most important aspect of the American continent before the poet has established any connection with it is

> Tierra mía sin nombre, sin América, . . .
> (i. 320)

This is reinforced in the following lines of the opening section, where the description of the continent before the poet builds his created world emphasizes that name and number are lacking. For Neruda, the name, the number of a man or a creature (i.e. quantity or size) place and define them in relation to larger schemes of classification:

> A las tierras sin nombres y sin números
> bajaba el viento desde otros dominios, . . .
> (i. 320)

Thus trees, animals, minerals are named, but behind each name there is the species to which it belongs, which in turn refers outwards still further to the substance it comes from, leading ultimately to *Tierra* or *Océano*.

This subject can only be touched upon here for purposes of demonstrating how it affects the organization of the instrumental sets; but it offers a whole subject of inquiry into the botanical, geological, and zoological fields of reference in the *Canto general*. Here the interest is mainly in the particular use that the instrumental sets serve in illustrating the thematic content of the poem, i.e. the various levels of reference that such connections imply.

To take an example: *árbol* is treated as a conceptual device to link various associated fields, i.e. the natural and the social; but Neruda also has a naturalist's interest in naming and classifying

THE POET AND THE COLLECTIVITY 27

all plants and creatures. Recalling the instrumental set *Hombre*⇌*Tierra* (see Fig. 1), we see that a process of increasing particularization occurs:

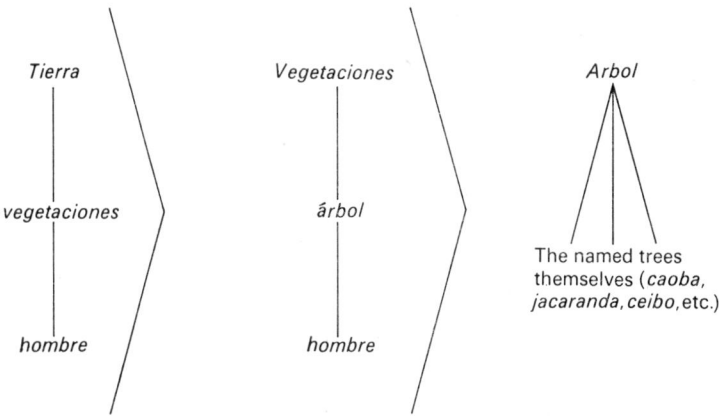

The progressive working from general instrumental set to particular named tree, and vice versa, is definitely linked, as is also the case with any particular beast, bird, or mineral (i. 320–34), or named social unit such as a tribe and country (i. 330–2).

In *Los libertadores* (i. 378–459) the named heroes are invoked for more than their revered memory; they imply a whole structure behind them, from name to *hombre* to *pueblo*, and from there to *árbol* as a conceptual device or to *tierra* as a whole, which is compared to the action of the particular named individual. Take for example the movement from general to particular, and vice versa, in *San Martín (1810)* (i. 407–9),[1] where the name of the man itself leads outwards to the earth itself:

> Eres la tierra que nos diste, un ramo
> de cedrón que golpea con su aroma,
> que no sabemos dónde está, de dónde
> llega su olor de patria a las praderas.
> Te galopamos, San Martín, salimos
> amaneciendo a recorrer tu cuerpo, . . .
>
> (i. 407)

[1] See also i. 450–3; here the relationship between named individuals and people as a whole is worked out in terms of *árbol–bosque*. Another example of this is i. 369:
> Se hicieron sombra los padres de piedra,
> se anudaron al bosque, . . .

This evidently links up with the *Hombre–Tierra, Cuerpo–Continente* sets (see Figs. 1, 2); but in this context it illustrates the movement of classification from named man to man as species (*Cuerpo*) to *Tierra*. The connection established, the poet mingles the body of the named man with the body of the continent in the now familiar fashion, ending with our death:

> Así sea, y que nos acompañe
> la paz hasta que entremos
> después de los combates, a tu cuerpo
> y duerma la medida que tuvimos
> en tu extensión de paz germinadora.
>
> (i. 409)

The shape of the man, the name of the man, the substance of the man are conceptually broken up and re-formed in a comparison with the earth itself. This can be viewed as a movement by the poet from the name of the man to the man as a member of a species, to a dismembering of this man and a progressive re-establishment of his form or totality on another plane, as the above lines plainly show.[1] The connections between *hombre* and *tierra* in the background as an instrumental set make this possible. This example should illustrate how the very name of a man, a creature, or an object implies a classificatory system designed to place somebody or something in relation to other men, or in relation to species of the same order. However, the systems of classification that refer out towards ever-increasing planes of generality are of interest in so far as they help to explain the description and definition of *hombre* and of the named *hombre* Pablo Neruda. The possibility that there exists a parallel with the classification devised by Linnaeus is but a tentative suggestion; further research might reveal a different type of system. However, in the *Canto general* it is no accident that the trees of *América* are named, that Neruda names in the *Canto general de Chile* (i. 528–52) trees, birds, plants (see especially 540–5). The instrumental sets establish how they are linked to

---

[1] In other words San Martín's anatomical shape as an individual man is taken to pieces and the parts of his body are compared to the parts of nature. When the poet brings the body back together he re-establishes the body or *cuerpo* on another plane, since the *cuerpo* of San Martín becomes the *cuerpo* of the continent or *Tierra*. A similar process occurs when San Martín's body is compared to the body of the collectivity or *pueblo*, which is also compared to *Tierra* (i. 407–9). See L.S., *The Savage Mind*, pp. 135–60.

man and to the poet, and how through their form and substance they suggest and explain man's relationship to nature and to other men (see also i. 680–1). It must be made clear that there is no hierarchy implied in the classification of the *Canto general*. The instrumental sets show the parts of nature related to *hombre*, and man as a creature amongst other living beings, but for Neruda there is no naturally pre-ordained 'chain of being' in which some men come above others. The naming of peoples and individuals is, then, a device to connect man to nature and to *Tierra*, to explain his origins by comparison with natural creatures and forms, whose continual existence around him implies his substance and origin. This enables the poet to work outwards from his own particular description and definition to the description and definition of man as a whole. The movement can be viewed as a passage from a species or group of species to a more general system of properties or categories. Frequently in the *Canto general* a device, like *árbol* or *mineral*, is used to take the movement from the level of species (be it man, or a bird, or a plant) upwards or outwards in the direction of *Tierra* or *Océano* (see Figs. 1, 3). This movement upwards or outwards on to planes of increasing generality contrasts with the movement downwards or inwards in the direction of proper names. Take for example the poem *Hacia los minerales* in *Las flores de Punitaqui* (i. 610–11): here the instrumental set *Hombre* ⇌ *Tierra* is isolated and progressively refined; then a mineral is named, and finally a man is named, giving us the final and most particular stage in this context:

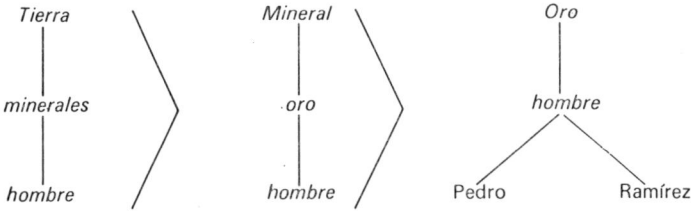

The shape of the man and the shape of metal are compared, and the shape of the continent as the ultimate general reference is compared (see Fig. 10) to the body of the man. The mundane, everyday actions of work and labour are given a profound and resonant dimension far beyond the particular context of the event. Furthermore, the relationship of the body of the continent and the body of man is described in male–female terms:

> ... ven,
> Pedro, con tu paz de cuero,
> ven, Ramírez, con tus abrasadas
> manos que indagaron el útero
> de las cerradas minerías, ...
> (i. 611)

The action of work and the action of producing gold from the interior of the continent suggest themes that will be dealt with in a later chapter. Here the point to be made is of the movement from the particular to the general, the reference outwards to *Cuerpo–Continente* and *tierra* through *oro* to *mineral* and finally to *tierra*. The natural organization and quality of the minerals in the earth are compared and contrasted with the men or *pueblo* who descend into the earth, back into their own origin and substance, to dig out the minerals (i. 610). The walls of the mines recall the walls of *Macchu-Picchu*:

> . . . . . .
> eran los dulces muros en que una
> piedra se amarra con otra,
> con un beso de barro oscuro. (i. 610)

The unity of the walls contrasts with the condition of the worker: these are social implications which relate back to *hombre*. The references attempt to explain the miners in terms of their descent into the uterus of the continent, as a descent into a structure which contrasts in some manner with that of their existence on the surface. In this piece the shape of the stones and the metals is both positive and negative. The work is both hard and painful for these men, but it is also ennobling and a symbol of their perpetual struggle. The work assumes a collective substance and shape, like the work of the men who built the city of Machu-Picchu. It is seen chiefly in reference back to the poet, who identifies with their work through his relationship to *Hombre–Tierra* as these men come up to become part of him, his *cuerpo*, his *palabra*, and his name.

Here the multiple devices operating show how the instrumental set in its simplicity gives way to a far more complex picture, where various logical comparisons are exploited at the same time:

(A) The form of man and the form of the continent.

THE POET AND THE COLLECTIVITY

(B) The action of going down into the mines, and the male entering the female form of the continent.

(C) The common substance of *Hombre* and *Tierra* that is implied in *Oro⇌Mineral*.

The movement of the piece shows remarkable affinities with *Alturas de Macchu-Picchu* (i. 335–48); indeed the whole of *Las flores de Punitaqui* (i. 607–20), with its autobiographical look backwards, and its description of the poet's discovery of his vocation as poet-spokesman in relation to others, is like the pattern of the more famous poem.[1] The comparison effected between the beauty and the form of the rose and the men themselves (i. 612) becomes fused into a form and substance which captures and retains in an image the collective agonies and aspirations of the men and the poet himself.

> Flores, flores de altura,
> flores de mina y piedra, flores (See Fig. 8c)
> de Punitaqui, hijas
> del amargo subsuelo: en mí, nunca olvidadas,
> quedasteis vivas, construyendo
> la pureza inmortal, una corola
> de piedra que no muere.
>
> (i. 612)

This recalls the same rose image in *Macchu-Picchu* (i. 341): indeed *Alturas de Macchu-Picchu* and *Las flores de Punitaqui* can be fruitfully compared, in the way that Neruda gets behind matter to man, and in the survey of his life looking both backward and forward:

> Antes anduve por la vida, en medio
> de un amor doloroso: antes retuve
> una pequeña página de cuarzo
> clavándome los ojos en la vida.[2]
>
> (i. 616)

---

[1] This fact has been noted by H. Loyola, 'Los modos de autoreferencia en la obra de Pablo Neruda', *Aurora*, 2ª epoca, No. 3–4 (July–Dec. 1964), pp. 36 ff. *Macchu-Picchu*, according to Loyola, was written in Aug.–Sept. 1945 in Isla Negra, but it was not published till 1946. In this year he also wrote *Punitaqui*, which is a direct result of his travels around Chile when he was campaigning for a seat in the Senate. See also H. Loyola's latest work, which contains in book form the ideas discussed, *Ser y morir en Pablo Neruda* (Santiago, 1967).

[2] The use of the word *cuarzo* or quartz means that the poet had not managed to retain the gold but only the quartz. This mineral, which generally crystallizes

But the movement of the section as a whole is even more striking, the movement up to the city and down into the earth, as in *Macchu-Picchu* (i. 339–40), behind the aspect of the mine and its metal to the essential substance of man, as it is revealed in the substance of the metal itself when it comes into contact with man. Furthermore, the labour in the mines is linked to the person of the poet whose task it is to speak for these men:

> Hermano de corazón quemado,
> junta en mi mano esta jornada,
> y bajemos una vez más a las capas dormidas
> en que tu mano como una tenaza
> agarró el oro que quería volar
> aún más profundo, aún más abajo, aún.
>
> (i. 611)

The coming together of men and metal is expressed in the shape and structure of the flower, and linked in substance to the enduring *piedra* which, as the stone of the Easter Island statue (i. 661–3), and the stone of *Macchu-Picchu* (i. 345–7), is one of the key substances in the *Canto general* to define and describe man's relationship to his environment. Likewise *oro* plays its role in this section and in the *Canto general* as a whole, where the changing meaning and value of gold, as matter touched by men or used by exploiters for different functions, leads through to the various interconnected themes of the poem. This compares with the significance that the stone of Rapa Nui and Machu-Picchu has on the social and historical level. Thus, all these substances and the forms they take in different parts of the *Canto general* can be referred back to the *Hombre–Tierra* instrumental set (Fig. 1). The comparison between these sections underlines the stages of generalization in the *Canto general*'s frame of reference, and the fact that the poem has an enduring set of connections, in the background of which the internal dispositions and relations are constantly rearranged in different

in hexagonal prisms, consists in pure form of silica or silicon dioxide. It is always found in conjunction with gold deposits, but it is not as valuable. This relationship between gold and quartz is also mapped out in i. 336:

> el hombre arruga el pétalo de la luz que recoge
> en los determinados manantiales marinos
> y taladra el metal palpitante en sus manos.
> Y pronto, entre la ropa y el humo, sobre la mesa hundida,
> como una barajada cantidad, queda el alma:
> cuarzo y desvelo, lágrimas en el océano . . .

parts of the poem into new relationships that do not destroy the instrumental set to which they relate back.

In the *Canto general* as a whole there is an overriding feeling of tension between the poet's own private and personal description as an individual in relation to an environment, and the description of men, the continent, and the environment as a whole. Obviously the private and the public are linked systematically and logically, as this chapter has already shown, but nevertheless, on any level of meaning, be it social or historical, there is a self-contained public and private relationship. Pablo Neruda the individual is related to *Tierra/Océano* (Figs. 1, 3), but *hombre* in general is related to *Tierra/Océano* as well, and the poet as an individual is part of *hombre* (Figs. 1 and 3). Therefore within the reference upwards to a general connection there is this dual quality, which has already been noted. In his use of *idioma*, for example, the poet's language becomes linked with the general language of the people for whom he speaks,[1] but his own language is separate as well. Nevertheless, it is also true to say that the collective experiences are described and illuminated by virtue of the individual experience of the poet himself (see especially i. 348). Although the poet works neatly from the particular event to the general framework, and vice versa, it does not obviate this feeling of dualism or tension, i.e. the concept that two strands are intertwined in any reference in the poem. First, the poet as a man defines and describes himself; and second, other men are defined and described. The two strands are, of course, connected by virtue of the fact that the poet is an individual within a larger whole, a man amongst other men. Nevertheless it is important to distinguish the strands as they present themselves in the poem. The poet is always the particular *hombre* of any context of the *Canto general*; that is, when the poem moves to any particular man, in the foreground is the named man Pablo Neruda, a man and part of *pueblo* and made up of *metal* and *piedra*.[2] It is this process which is crucial in *La lámpara en la tierra* (i. 319–34) and *Alturas de Macchu-Picchu* (i. 335–48), in *El gran océano* (i. 654–92), and *Las flores de Punitaqui* (i. 607–20), as this chapter has demonstrated; and it is this process which operates in any part of

[1] See page 6, where we spoke of the double use of *por*. This clarifies what we mean. People speak *for* him and *through* him, i.e. in some ways it can be viewed as something which occurs outside and independently of the poet, but in another sense it is something which occurs within the poet as spokesman for others.

[2] Monegal, op. cit., pp. 246–9.

the *Canto general*. By defining man as a whole, the poet defines and describes himself as well. It is important, however much one emphasizes the general and social framework, to remember the degree of personal and emotional involvement, and therefore in every case how the context of any part of the poem relates back to *hombre* and to the poet's person in particular. However, *hombre* and Pablo Neruda are two distinct, though related, entities. The poet is an individual whose anatomical form is a self-contained system of parts, but he is a member of a species who collectively make up *pueblo* or *hombre* in general. This species as a collectivity is in turn a system connected with *Tierra/Océano* (Figs. 1, 3). The form of the body can be used as a conceptual device to link up all these entities, but that does not eradicate this dualism. Neruda can describe himself, he can talk about himself, whilst all the time implying his connection with *Hombre*⇌*Tierra/Océano* and men in general. Conversely, he can speak about nature and men in general whilst implying himself. Thus in every case Neruda is defining himself as well as others, but the two strands are related, in the sense that he is one of the others as well as himself. It is the existence of other people, and their experiences as human beings, that enrich the life of Pablo Neruda and consequently materially affect his poetry. When this relates back to the parts in the instrumental sets it can be seen that the poet's form receives and synthesizes all the elements that are classified, flowing from *Tierra* and *Océano* in every case; therefore, the parts of a whole are regrouped within the poet's form. The poet's relation to the collectivity is now clearly defined in the light of these two main devices that operate throughout the *Canto general*.

First, there are the instrumental sets, which are finite. Their structure is simple, but the number of elements that can be incorporated into them is limitless, although in practice it is defined by the structure of the poem itself. With these classificatory schemes Neruda is able to classify and relate to man the whole framework of nature, so that all the parts of the natural order are used to describe and define man.

Second, within the poem he isolates an instrumental set at a particular connection, in order to utilize it to make interconnected references about man on a social and historical level. When Neruda moves up the instrumental set, this merely implies that he moves from the individual or particular event on to planes of increasing generality, which are implied by the isolated part of any instrumental set. The part that is isolated is used to compare man with a natural or man-made form, in both its shape and substance, moving from the particular context to a general proposition (such as the death of men in the shape and substance of the stone). This Neruda is able to do by virtue of the fact that he can use the instrumental set as a framework of reference to appeal to in any context.

This chapter has shown, first, that it is a question of placing the stone, tree, or wave in some natural context, and defining its relationship to man in terms of a general system; and that, furthermore, this general system moves down on to the most particular category, to the very names of plants and minerals in the poem. Second, it has demonstrated in detail the use of stone, tree, or wave as images that logically work out the themes of the poem on various levels of meaning, or on general interconnected planes of reference. Therefore the first question deals with a classification of nature into some kind of order or pattern, and the second has to do with the use made of these natural forms, in a logical and conceptual way, as images to illustrate the themes of the poem. Because of the two points examined here certain substances in the *Canto general*, such, for example, as *piedra* and *oro*, are important both for their place in the natural scheme of things, and also as devices, once their place has been defined, to illustrate some aspect of *hombre*: the relationship between man-made forms and forms found in nature, and the emphasis on natural substances used by man, take the *Canto general* into a well-defined set of comparisons between nature and culture. The movement from nature to culture explains the origin of man and his make-up, and this fact is implied in any reference back, right through to *Tierra/Océano*. Furthermore, in his social organization, in explaining and understanding himself, man builds social systems which are made up of comparisons effected between plants, metals, and creatures which are both natural and logical. They are natural because they occupy a preordained place in nature, and they are logical because men structure them into concepts which are of their own making, but which are based on the parts of nature. The imagery in the *Canto general* does two things: (*a*) In the instrumental sets it defines and describes in the most general terms the place of man in relation to nature. (*b*) In any particular context of the poem, the images used are parts of these sets, and they link man and nature in a logical way. The poetry of the *Canto general* celebrates this connection between man's cultural forms, which are man-made, and the natural forms, there long before men. But the images are now used to convey facts which are not natural but logical in relation to the instrumental sets. This distinction might be taken by some to beg the question that the organization of a poem's imagery must be logical in some way, but the point here is that, when talking about the connections between nature and culture (culture in the sense of men's work and activity, both physical and spiritual), the connections established in the instrumental set are natural, in that they describe and place plants and metals in their context of reality, whereas to talk about these forms when they are used as images in a poem implies that they are being used logically, as part of the organization of the poem's structure.

The word 'natural' implies the place of an object or creature in the poet's scheme of things, in which he aims to name it and to relate it to a species. Once this has been achieved, the poet can use it as a conceptual device with multiple possibilities to define and describe man.[1] It is these possibilities which constitute the poet's themes in the *Canto general*. Although it is proposed to divide them into interconnected planes of reference, within each plane, say the social or historical plane, there is a self-contained movement from the particular to the general. The key factor in Pablo Neruda's poetry is the way that some of these images, used long before the *Canto general*, have taken on additional levels of meaning or reference outside the poet's own personal situation. This is what makes the *Canto general* a poem at the same time so personal and so epic in its view of men.

[1] See L.S., *The Savage Mind*, pp. 148–9.

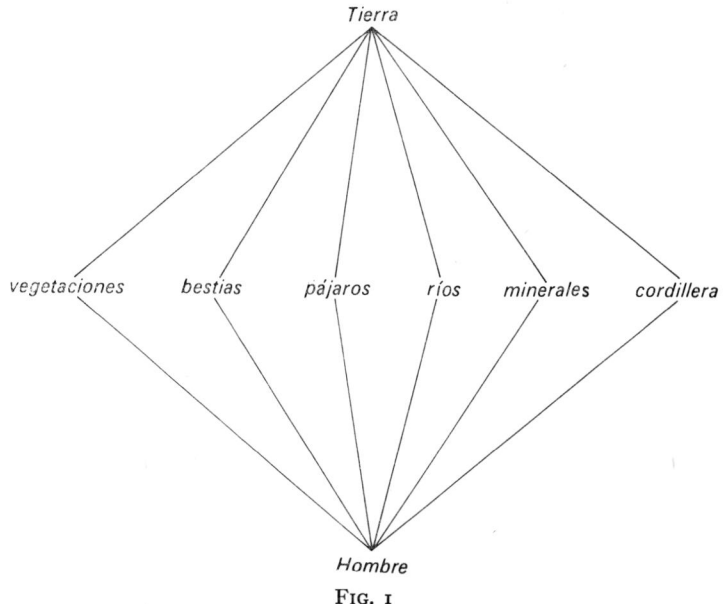

Fig. 1

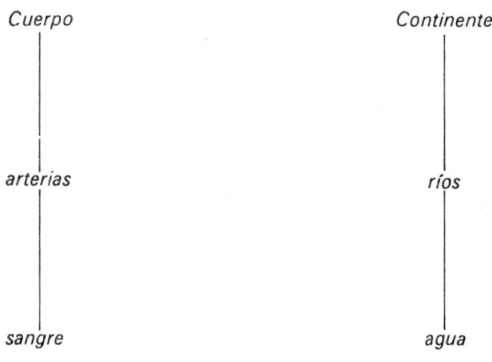

Fig. 2

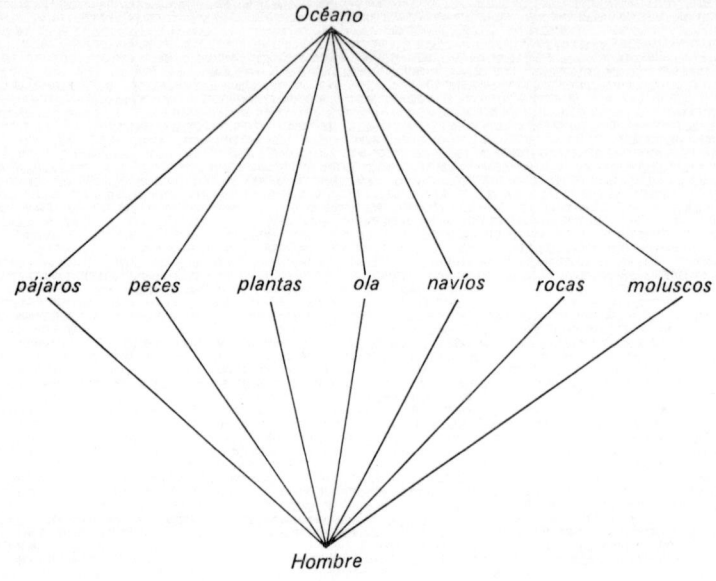

Fig. 3

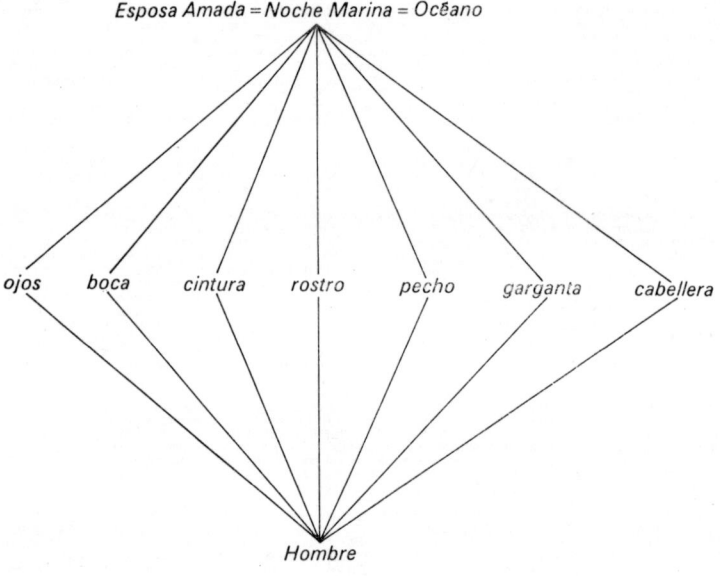

Fig. 4

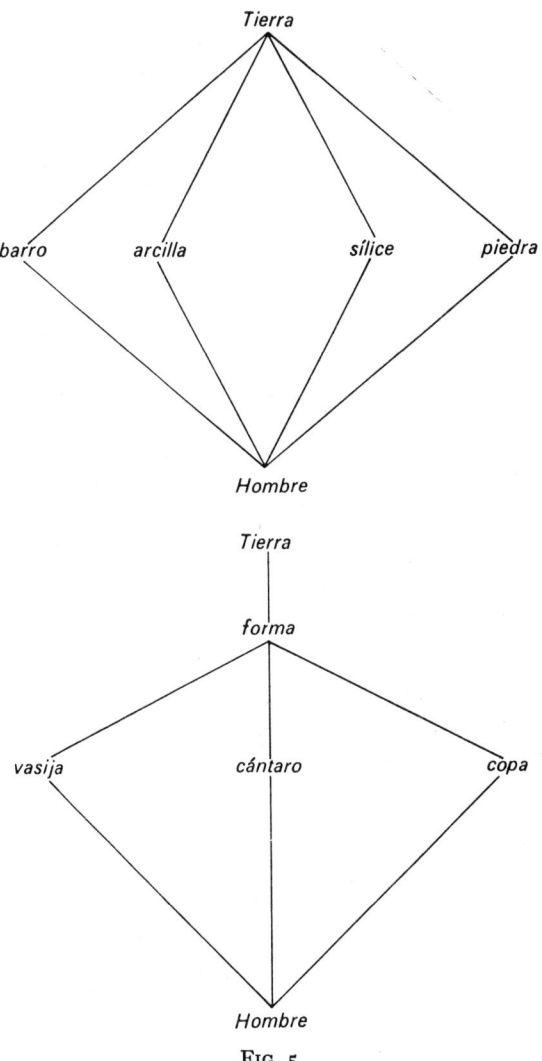

Fig. 5

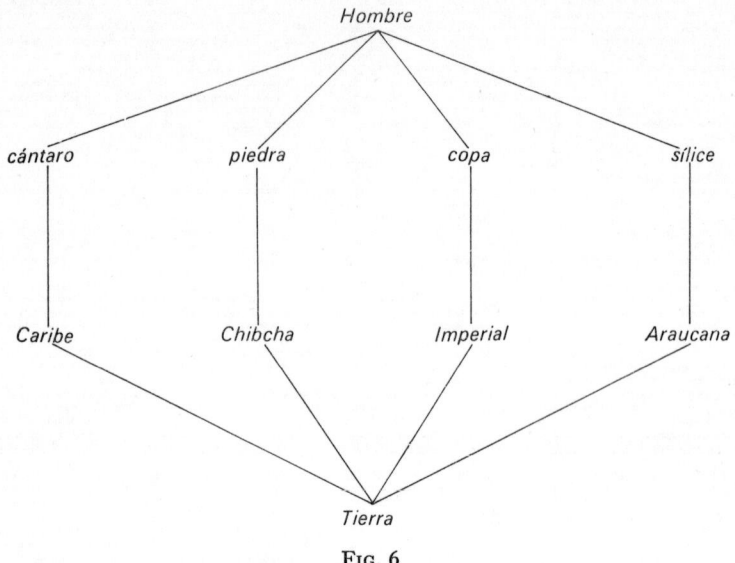

Fig. 6

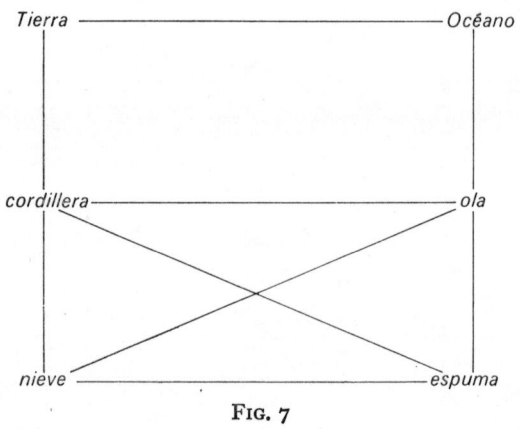

Fig. 7

THE POET AND THE COLLECTIVITY

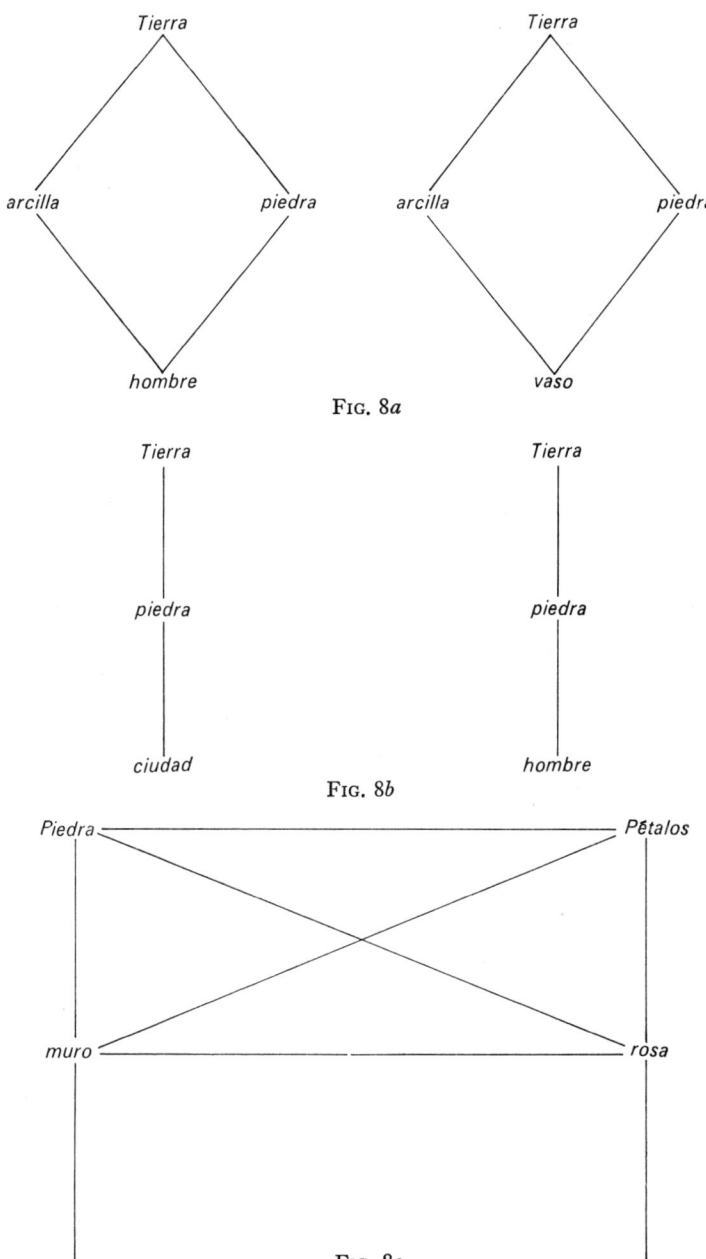

Fig. 8a

Fig. 8b

Fig. 8c

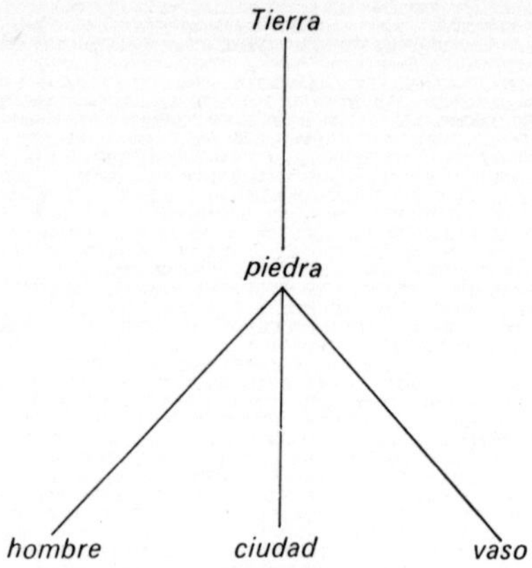

THE POET AND THE COLLECTIVITY

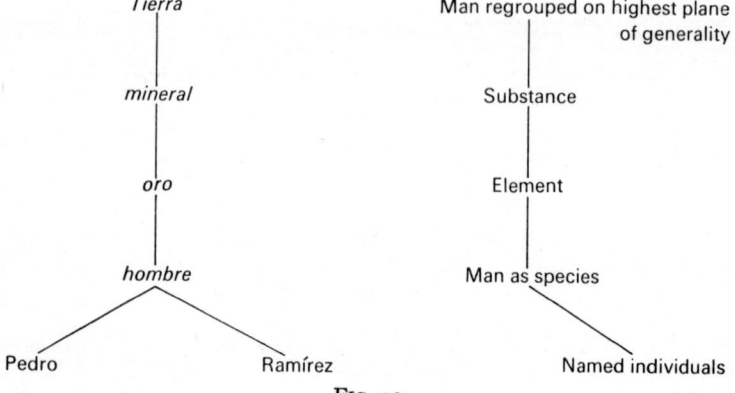

FIG. 8d

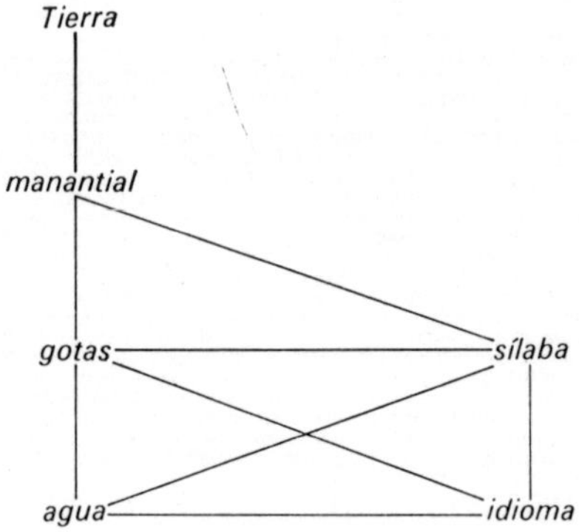

FIG. 9

FIG. 10

II

THE NATURAL PLANE OF REFERENCE

THIS chapter is concerned with the discernible levels of meaning that the imagery refers to; in other words it involves a discussion of the poem's field of reference. The last chapter introduced the clear-cut devices that the poet employs in his use of images, enabling him to relate them to larger entities outside his own individual body and particular existence.

Having attempted to define and describe this movement, and how Neruda uses the shape and substance of man, and the shapes and substances of nature, as logical or conceptual devices to effect this movement, it is now possible to describe the various levels or planes of reference as embodied in the structured and organized images of the poem. This has not altogether been ignored; more than once in the previous chapter it has been impossible to talk about techniques and devices without mentioning to some extent the themes that the poetry deals with, be they individual, social, historical, or any other. Now that the argument has led through specifically to the imagery of the *Canto general*, a crucial issue will have to be noted: should a critical analysis examine the *Canto general* as a whole, or should it take into account the changing circumstances of composition? By this it is meant that the development of the poem over a period of years may have affected the growth of the poet's themes, and consequently the precise reference and essential meaning of the images may have changed. Should a distinction be made, for example, between poems written before *Alturas de Macchu-Picchu* and those written after?[1] Clearly this is very important, since Neruda's experiences in this fortress-city and his re-creation of them in a long poem materially affected his subsequent work. Viewing the *Canto general* as a continuing growth over a period of time would make it well, nigh impossible, to

---

[1] H. Loyola, *Ser y morir en P.N.*, pp. 234 ff. See ii. 1360–6. Here Loyola lists poems published before 1950 that were incorporated into the *Canto general*. This is a valuable guide to the sequence of composition.

examine it as a whole, since the poem would have become a collection of loosely connected poems on various themes which vaguely resembled one another. Neruda's personal experiences from 1936 to 1950 in Spain, Mexico, and Chile have undoubtedly affected the scope and length of the work; but in order to speak in a meaningful way about the *Canto general* it is necessary to treat the finished work as it would appear to the reader once it had been written. This means that it should be considered as a finished product, where the sequence of composition, and the sequence of impact on a reader once a work has been written, are two different things.

In examining over-all themes of the *Canto general*, we must take care that the discussion of particular passages does not divorce images from their context, and attribute references that are external to their meaning in that particular poem. Any commentary examines how the imagery works outwards to major themes and relationships which are recurrent in the poem as a whole. It is important to note that the particular and personal emotion of the poet, together with his intellectual reaction to the land and its past, crystallizes in a set of images culled from his view of the continent's geography and history. For the poet, a set of objects and their natural origins and substance, or a chain of events, becomes the formula for that particular emotion; but it is the structured images themselves when they are formulated, not the emotion itself, which is the field of inquiry. An examination of the structure and organization of the imagery, such as we have already begun, leads us outwards to the larger over-all themes of the poem, which are present at various levels in any part of the *Canto general*. Consequently the imagery becomes something which contains in a tangible form the interior emotion of the poet and the external reference of the poem. Such a method helps us to view all levels of reference in the poem in an integral manner. By this it is meant that nature, man, history, society, are obviously enough all related, and if one has a particular action in one compartment, it is bound to have repercussions in all others. This is quite clear in all levels of reference in the *Canto general*. In the last chapter it was pointed out how the essential tension of the poetry in the *Canto general* derives from the *dualism* between the poet's individual emotion and experience, and his incorporation of this individuality into a wider context which exists outside him. This long poem speaks of historical events, social action, and the movement of nature all

THE NATURAL PLANE OF REFERENCE 45

at the same time, and attempts to gather up these events in the person of Pablo Neruda. And yet Neruda is at pains to demonstrate how he is one amongst many; hence the importance of the word *por* in the closing lines of *Alturas de Macchu-Picchu* (i. 348). When plotting the various levels of reference in the *Canto general* it will be important to understand the coming together of the individual context of the poet, and the cultural context of the poem's field of reference, as an analysis tries to break it down into its component levels. Here the term 'culture' is used in its widest sense, combining the physical lives of people and the spiritual concepts which arise out of their place in an environment, where they utilize the elements or parts of nature to describe themselves. Therefore it is the personal as it flows into the cultural stream that should be noted in examining the field of reference in the *Canto general*. Culture can be defined as follows:

> The genuine culture ... is the expression of a richly varied and yet somehow unified and consistent attitude toward life, an attitude which sees the significance of any one element of civilization in relation to all others. It is, ideally speaking, a culture in which nothing is spiritually meaningless, in which no important part of the general functioning brings with it a sense of frustration, of misdirected or unsympathetic effort. It is not a spiritual hybrid of contradictory patches, of watertight compartments of consciousness that avoid participation in a harmonious synthesis.[1]

It is this integral feeling about a genuine culture, stressed by this passage, a way of life where the spiritual and material aspects are harmoniously fused for a collectivity in a particular environment, which is of interest to the argument of this study. This notion is at the centre of the *Canto general*, we find, when considering its over-all meaning. A key factor in the development of Pablo Neruda's imagery is the way in which recurring images, used for many years, have taken on additional levels of meaning in the *Canto general*. As a result, no commentary seeks to locate the meaning of an image in the emotion of the poet; it seeks, rather, to clarify the outward field of reference of the *Canto general* as embodied in the imagery.

In order to illustrate this point, what follows is a general

---

[1] Edward Sapir, *Culture, Language and Personality* (Berkeley, Calif., 1966), p. 90.

commentary on seventeen lines of Poem III in *Canto general de Chile* (i. 533). However, reference will be made to the preceding poems, *Himno y regreso* (1939) (i. 529–30) and *Quiero volver al Sur* (1941) (i. 530–1), which are Poems I and II respectively. Here is the extract that we examine in a little more detail:

> No sólo el aire agudo del vegetal me espera:
> no sólo el trueno sobre el nevado esplendor:
> lágrimas y hambres como dos escalofríos
> suben al campanario de la patria y repican:
> de ahí que en medio del fragante cielo,   5
> de ahí que cuando Octubre estalla, y corre
> la primavera antártica sobre el fulgor del vino,
> hay un lamento y otro y otro lamento y otro
> hasta que cruzan nieve, cobre, caminos, naves
> y pasan a través de la noche y la tierra   10
> hasta mi desangrada garganta que los oye.
> Pueblo mío, qué dices? Marinero,
> peón, alcalde, obrero del salitre, me escuchas?
> Yo te oigo, hermano muerto, hermano vivo; te oigo,
> lo que tú deseabas, lo que enterraste, todo,   15
> la sangre que en la arena y en el mar derramabas,
> el corazón golpeado que resiste y asusta.   (i. 533)

Here the poet reaches a climax in his formal address to *patria* or *Sur* as he calls it in this extract. This commentary shows how the South, which is evoked at a distance by the poet, is built up of the familiar and recurrent elements of his vision of nature. There is, as it were, a certain standardization of the 'landscape', which leads the poet through to other levels of reference. Man's unhappy and imperfect social condition is connected to the landscape emitting cries on behalf of *pueblo*, a collectivity which is both a part of nature and its logical climax. In other words, the rhythm and voice of nature are harnessed to the rhythm and voice of the people, and the voice of nature, as it becomes the voice of suffering sailors and workers, is heard by the poet. Therefore the reader is taken in a movement from nature to the poet, through a creation of art. This last sentence can be expanded to mean the poet's emotional experience as it has taken form, translated into an external landscape built up of discernible images which are outside the poet and accessible to us, which becomes nature recreated in art.[1] Since

[1] See F. Schwartzmann, *El sentimiento de lo humano en América* (Santiago, 1953), especially pp. 143–72 ('Del sentimiento de la naturaleza.').

THE NATURAL PLANE OF REFERENCE

it was shown earlier how the poet uses clear-cut formal devices and techniques to open his personal emotion into an external and general panorama, an analysis may now plot the meaning or reference. The poet, in this extract, arrives at a social and historical description of the people in Chile through the logical use of selected parts of nature. The opening lines of this poem, *Melancolía cerca del Orizaba* (1942) (i. 531), have stated the question:

> Qué hay para ti en el Sur sino un río, una noche,
> unas hojas que el aire frío manifiesta
> y extiende hasta cubrir las riberas del cielo?

The answer will be that these elements of the landscape, *río, noche, hojas, cielo*, will acquire a power of reference that evokes the human beings, within nature, who cry out. Not only those who are alive, but those who are dead speak to the poet, i.e. the past and the present exist in the synchronic structure of nature which contains all time up to the present. These various possibilities of interpretation make up in their synthesis the integral view of the environment mentioned earlier. Lines 1–7 describe a panorama made up of *aire, vegetal, trueno, nevado esplendor*, etc., within which the cries of people manifest themselves. The repetition of *no sólo* is balanced by the repetition of *de ahí*. The importance of such phrases for mobilizing the argument of the poem is clear; to invoke them is a common device in the *Canto general*, as in Section XI of *Alturas de Macchu-Picchu*, where the word *déjame* is constantly repeated (i. 346). Here, however, the *vegetal* and the *trueno* lead us through to hunger and the sound of crying; and the hunger and the voice of these people in their misery give the poet a chance to bring out the contrast between the natural and the social. Thunder, i.e. noise, leads to noise of crying; and vegetable, i.e. food, leads to denial of vegetable in life, i.e. hunger. In other words, these elements of nature are used here with a definite human or social reference. The sound of the people collectively crying out in the midst of this landscape is conveyed by the bell image in line 4. The bell image ringing out a human cry contrasts with earlier references to *campana*, when the poet addresses *patria* in terms of its natural phenomena:

> Voy a escoger la flora delgada del nitrato,
> voy a hilar el estambre glacial de la campana, . . .
>
> (i. 530)

The bell image in the *Canto general* is frequently used to convey the spreading of news, or it may be a movement signifying the passing of someone, whose death, reported everywhere, ensures that the struggle will be carried on by others.

> . . . . . .
> Hidalgo cae, Morelos recoge
> el sonido, el temblor de una campana
> propagado en la tierra y en la sangre.
> (i. 422)

A similar example is to be found in *A Silvestre Revueltas*:

> Desde hoy tu nombre lleno de música volará
> cuando se toque tu patria, como desde una campana, . . .
> (i. 632)

These examples show *campana* fulfilling a historical function as well as a social one, i.e. the bell ringing symbolizes *patria* in a human sense when the people who make up the collectivity cry out. In this passage, *campana* has moved from a part of the description of *patria* where it is silent and a part of nature, to its use as the bell that carries human voices out of nature.[1] In the very poem that we are looking at there is a reference to *campana*, where its shape is the shape of a plant in nature, either the *copihue*, a flower native to and often invoked to symbolize Chile, or the well-known *campanilla*: 'Flor cuya corola es de una pieza, y de *figura de campana*, que producen la enredadera y otras plantas.'[2] The movement of this whole poem is conveyed in the various levels of reference implied by *campana*. Here is the full quotation:

> . . . .
> y el brillo de la lluvia cierra su enredadera
> desde la reunión de los granos secretos
> hasta el follaje lleno de campanas y gotas?
> (i. 531)

The meaning and value of nature in itself are an important reference, but the use of *campana* in this context, and its use earlier, fore-

---

[1] It still remains, however, to describe the outline of *patria* in line 4: *campanario de la patria*.
[2] See Real Academia Española, *Diccionario de la lengua española* (Madrid, 1956). The dictionary definition of *campanilla* quoted contains my own italics.

THE NATURAL PLANE OF REFERENCE

shadows the key role it has in line 4 of our commentary extract. Let us set out the three references side by side:

(1) el estambre glacial de la campana
(i. 530)

(2) follaje lleno de campanas y gotas
(i. 531)

(3) lágrimas y hambres como dos escalofríos
suben al campanario de la patria y repican: ...
(i. 533)

This movement usefully serves to draw some initial conclusions: First, the shapes of natural objects are evoked primarily for their natural reference, for their life and beauty as part of the natural environment, but also for the meaning that they present to the poet as a wider reference, as to the whereabouts of man in any landscape. Second, it works through to the sound of human voices in the actual image of the bell ringing, and the tears of *pueblo* hark back to the natural picture 'follaje lleno de campanas y gotas'. Thus *gotas* leads to *lágrimas*, where *gotas* are the raindrops on the surface of the flower. The rain of nature, which falls on the plant, becomes the tears of people who suffer social misery. The plant covered with water is the bell which rings out their tearful condition to the poet. The natural reference contains a human and social one, and the movement is all brought together in the *campana* image. The poet not only describes in a disinterested manner the beauty and meaning of nature, therefore, but the anguish, the inhumanity of social conditions that can be discovered in any landscape of Chile: hence the answer to Neruda's question earlier,

Qué hay para ti en el Sur sino un río, ...

is contained in *no sólo* of lines 1 and 2 of our extract.

The many cries signify the coming together of the individual experiences into the social or collective reality, and also a historical reality, the presence of the past. This is illustrated by the crucial list in line 9, where the synthesis of human cries engendered by social injustice brings together and organizes the synthesis of nature or *patria* as a whole. Thus *patria* can be broken up and regrouped by use of formal elements that comprise it, e.g. *lluvia, campana, hojas*, etc., seen on several interconnected planes of reference. It is this movement, above all, which this analysis attempts to show. The *patria* as a whole now contains the cries of the *pueblo*, a collective whole which balances the whole of *patria*, evoked in terms of its diversity:

> . . . .
> hasta que cruzan nieve, cobre, caminos, naves, . . .

The contrast between land and sea is a perennial one in Neruda's poetry when describing Chile: mountains and waves, and, by analogy, snow and foam, are familiar pairs of contrasts that abound in the *Canto general* when Chile is mentioned (see Fig. 7). Take for example the lines of *Himno y regreso* (1939) which just precede the passage extracted:

> Patria, mi patria
> toda rodeada de agua combatiente
> y nieve combatida, . . .
>
> (i. 530)

Here, in line 9, the contrast to describe *patria* is *nieve/naves*. The *patria* is welded together in the sound of the bell, which carries the sound of human voices into and through everything in nature, e.g. *nieve, cobre, caminos, naves*. The reference outward to *Tierra/Océano* is evident, and this whole sound and totality is poured into the vessel of the poet in line 11. Evidently the *patria*, made up of parts of nature, is incomplete if one does not include the people within it, and the manner in which nature and man affect one another.[1] The sound of the people becomes the sound of the poet's voice, as the contrast between the two, speech and sound, implies. The poet hears the sound, the poet speaks the cry. The sound of the people's cry is carried over America by the bell, through the air and through the land, shared by all, to the poet who is in a foreign land. The pouring of these people's cries into the body of the poet means that *pueblo* will live again, and give life and voice to all their desires and hopes through the art of the poet. The *desangrada garganta* of line 11 links through to the imagery of line 16, where the blood of these people spills away into the for-

---

[1] See Schwartzmann, op. cit., p. 166: 'Quizás podría decirse que la armonía dada entre el hombre y la tierra sólo se consigue cuando el desnivel y distanciamiento existente entre el paisaje natural y la visión cultural es de tal magnitud, que, por decirlo así, uno de los extremos — acaso el paisaje cultural — reduce a casi nada al otro.'

THE NATURAL PLANE OF REFERENCE

gotten past and into the death of the sea. The list of people addressed is paralleled by the nouns listed in line 9, since the sea, the soil, and the mines (*naves, caminos, cobre*) are represented by *marinero, peón, obrero de salitre*. The list of nature connects with the list of men who have some work in transforming and handling nature. The poet tries to communicate back with them, and the natural plane of reference which led through to a social one, all gathered together in the person of the poet, admits a further historical plane of reference. As in any poem of the *Canto general*, the poet identifies himself totally both with the past, and with living men and their unfulfilled aspirations conveyed in lines 15–16. *Hermanos* both living and dead become *sangre en la arena* and *en el mar*. Note again this key contrast, when the poet is creating a landscape of nature with its layers of meaning, between land and sea. The permanence of death suggests itself in the blood in the sea, whereas the social injustice and cruelty of treatment that *pueblo* receives are suggested by blood spilt over and sucked in by the arid and hostile sand of the north of Chile, where the *salitre* fields are to be found.

Such a passage shows the levels of reference in any part of the *Canto general* which are played out in the images that the poet employs. Furthermore, the imagery as a structured organization reveals fields of reference which are considerably more accessible than in earlier poetry by Neruda. It is a question of seeing how the individual becomes easier to locate when he describes himself in social and historical context, or, to use an over-all term, a cultural frame of reference. These additional layers of meaning that enrich the recurrent images in Neruda's poetry now point towards definite social or historical events which occurred in the past, or which the poet has experienced for himself in the present. These events, and totalities such as *patria* or *pueblo*, are given a highly individual and personal interpretation in terms of the particular vision of the natural environment to which Neruda conforms. The commentary has served to illustrate how it is necessary to separate the various planes of reference, even though they are interconnected or implied in any one particular instance. This was the case in the previous chapter. For when the Araucanians struggle to defend their territory or *patria*, they are defending every aspect of their culture in a physical and spiritual sense; it is a defence on the natural, social, historical, and individual planes at one and the same time, played out in the use of shapes and substances of nature as imagery (i. 367–71). The strength of the *Canto general* derives from this coherent and integral view of life, which enables the poet to refer with confidence to the Continent as a whole, or to *patria*, by the formal use of images which contain this larger reference. In the *Canto general*, therefore, the description of nature, its use and abuse by man, the existence of man within this natural framework, the social group that man builds up, and his historical continuity with the past, are all woven together into a texture of astonishing richness in its field of reference. These many strands are a definition of Neruda's notion of an *American* culture mentioned earlier. This is the key problem of the individual context and the cultural context, how the poet's personal experience reaches out to embrace or take in the collective or shared experiences of a whole Continent. The problem has its literary aspects, in the sense of shared literary conventions or traditions. In other words, future inquiries should seek to determine to what extent some of the references in the *Canto general* are to formal or stylized themes inherited from previous American literature. The question of the individual and the cultural should also be examined in this form.

To exemplify this integral view of a culture and its component parts all leading from one to another, there is a rare and rewarding statement made by Neruda on the subject of *La Araucana* which corresponds very closely to a definition of the *Canto general*. His opinion about the former clearly indicates certain views that were instrumental in the creation of the latter:

> En *La Araucana* no vemos sólo el épico desarrollo de hombres trabados en un combate mortal, no sólo la valentía y la agonía de nuestros padres abrazados en el común exterminio, sino también la palpitante catalogación forestal y natural de nuestro patrimonio. Aves y plantas, aguas y pájaros, costumbres y ceremonias, idiomas y cabelleras, flechas y fragancias, nieve y mareas que nos pertenecen, *todo esto tuvo nombre*, por fin, en *La Araucana* y *por razón del verbo comenzó a vivir*. Y esto que recibimos como un legado sonoro era nuestra existencia que debíamos preservar y defender.[1]

Here, the inherited literary tradition and its continuity with the past preserve the totality of an integral and harmonious culture.

---

[1] P.N., *Discursos*, p. 62 (my italics).

THE NATURAL PLANE OF REFERENCE 53

Customs and ceremonies derive from substances of nature and its creatures, and Neruda refers to the diversity of this environment with the usual catalogue of familiar images, within which classification, naming, and description are important tasks, as the previous chapter illustrated. The shape of this *patrimonio* is seen in terms of *nieve y mareas*, a related pair of opposites which are quite standard.[1] Furthermore, Neruda refers to the historical survival of this totality in literature, history, and nature. It survives in nature because the natural flora and fauna survive today, and it survives in literature both because of language that can describe and name the plants and rivers, and because it can be eternally re-created in art. Again, one is led back to nature and its re-creation in art, a point mentioned earlier. This passage provides us with an admirable synthesis of all the elements of the Nerudian landscape and its special meaning in relation to *hombre* as a collectivity, i.e. *pueblo*. The two when they come together constitute that *legado sonoro* to be examined in detail further on. In order to explain all this properly it becomes necessary to examine the relation of man to nature, both in terms of his life and death in nature and in terms of his origins. Then it will be possible to describe Neruda's conception of man in an elaborately structured and organized cosmology.

The central meaning and value of nature in the poetry of Neruda are without question, but his development as a poet is reflected in his changing and increasingly wide view of nature in relation to man. The contrast between the earth and the sea provides a fundamental opposition, around which the themes of the *Canto general* are structured. This frame of reference has already been introduced in the two basic instrumental sets of the *Canto general*: *Hombre* ⇌ *Tierra* and *Hombre* ⇌ *Océano*. The origins of man in nature are the first principle in the whole poem; history is a movement away from this origin, and socially the conflicts of groups are the use and abuse of nature by individuals, together with their struggle to regain contact with nature or their true origin, perverted by unjust social forms. In order to comprehend fully the social and historical themes, then, it becomes necessary to describe Neruda's

[1] This exchange of attributes is a recurring pattern when Neruda describes *patria*; the continual mingling of *mar-tierra*, *nieve-espuma* (see Fig. 7). is reminiscent of Calderón and Góngora This is important to an understanding of the imagery.

view of the forces of nature as they relate to man, since these form the background to the whole frame of reference in the *Canto general*.

Hombre, as described in the *Canto general*, at the most profound level contains within him the forces of life and death; these are played out at the level of nature by the conflict of land and sea. This, for example, is contained, as already suggested, in the continual reference to *patria* in terms of land and sea, mountains and waves, snow and foam (see Fig. 7). Furthermore, it enables the poet to build up a field of related pairs of opposites, which become interchangeable, and contain this profound suggestion of life and death in any natural, social, or historical description of *patria*. When man moves away from the basic death of nature, he also removes himself from the life of nature and enters the social life within which his death and his sufferings are engendered by other men. Life and death become, therefore, no longer a sequence in a meaningful natural pattern, but the horrible anguished daily death of everyday social misery.[1] The true and essential forces of nature are compared to the social imperfections, and serve to remind man that his social and historical forms began in nature:

> Mazatlán estrellado, puerto de noche, escucho
> las olas que golpean tu pobreza
> y tus constelaciones, ... (i. 671)

The natural force of the waves hitting the land which survives their action reminds the poet that the poverty of the port is socially motivated or man-made. The positive aspects of society are those that harness themselves to the meaning and movement of these natural elements and forces in an integral culture.

It is important to realize how these themes have developed from Neruda's earlier poetry, where the inability to confront death in any proper sense led the poet to express a seemingly insoluble dilemma. The poetry written between 1925 and 1935[2] seemed to express this dilemma in the shape of questions which Neruda could not answer, as in *Galope muerto*, for example (i. 174):

> Ahora bien, de qué está hecho ese surgir de palomas
> que hay entre la noche y el tiempo, como una barranca húmeda?
> Ese sonido ya tan largo

---

[1] Here we have also to consider the origins of man and his movement from the sea to the land, where he builds his social and historical existence.
[2] See *Residencia en la tierra*, i and ii (1925–35), i. 173–253.

que cae listando de piedras los caminos,
más bien, cuando sólo una hora
crece de improviso, extendiéndose sin tregua.

(*Residencia en la tierra*, i)

These questions which the poetry sought to answer were to do with the poet's life, which was fleeting and personal, a movement through a daily death to an eternal death, which could not be linked to the eternal and impassive flow or flight of nature. Neruda was greatly concerned, also, to decipher for himself the mystery of the birth of life, seen, for example, as a sound which sets time in motion and causes it to start expanding towards an end which he could not understand. The major image for all these questions resolved itself in the sea, which conveyed the sense of accumulated time acquiring a silence and stillness of eternity.[1] There are two types of death in Neruda's poetry: the daily death, and the eternal death of nature conveyed by the sea and expressed in the collective death of the men of Machu-Picchu. The first is the daily death of events, the drop-drop of one hour to the next, from day to day, the inability to define a purpose and relation to everyday life. The second, represented by silence and immobility, and the accumulation of layers of time which seem to carry a man nowhere, is the death in nature, which Neruda understands eventually through his development of man in a historical dimension.[2] This enables Neruda to understand death as having some meaning, because a meaningless view of death gives no meaning to life, since it is flowing towards a meaningless goal. Neruda had to find how life was reborn, or lived on in others, before he could come to such a conclusion.

All these general remarks are crucial to understanding the profound level of meaning in the *Canto general* as it becomes translated into visible social and historical events, which are based on this view of nature and man. The poet wrote a key essay on this subject which deals with the poetry of Quevedo as it affected his view of life and death. This extract shows the relevance of the preceding remarks:

Hay una sola enfermedad que mata, y ésa es la vida. Hay un solo paso, y es el camino hacia la muerte. Hay una manera sola de gasto y de

---

[1] See A. Alonso, *Poesía y estilo de Pablo Neruda*, 3rd edn. (Buenos Aires, 1966), which discusses this question in some detail with respect to *Residencia en la tierra*.   [2] See H. Loyola, *Los modos* . . ., pp. 31 ff.

mortaja, es el paso arrastrador del tiempo que nos conduce. Nos conduce adónde? Si al nacer empezamos a morir, si cada día nos acerca a un límite determinado, si la vida misma es una etapa patética de la muerte, si el mismo minuto de brotar avanza hacia el desgaste del cual la hora final es sólo la culminación de ese transcurrir, no integramos la muerte en nuestra cuotidiana existencia, no somos parte perpetua de la muerte, no somos lo más audaz, lo que ya salió de la muerte? No es lo más mortal, lo más viviente, por su mismo misterio? . . . Si ya hemos muerto, si venimos de la profunda crisis, perderemos el temor a la muerte. Si el paso más grande de la muerte es el nacer, el paso menor de la vida es el morir.[1]

Therefore, the first notion to get clear is that the forces of life and death are inside man from the very start, and that he emerges to be born out of death and to re-enter death when he dies. But what meaning does all this metaphysical speculation lead to? Here it is impossible to answer this question without stating that *hombre* has an important distinction which sets him apart from nature. Although man has his origins in, and is part of, nature, unlike the organisms of nature he has a history[2] which lives on in the present. Although he is a natural and temporal being, he is also a historical being, who is always renewing himself with the past which lives on in the essence and spirit of the natural order. This gives Neruda a chance to hope for man, because it gives him some meaning in the daily flow of events which he lacked before. Death in the real sense has not been eliminated or glossed over, far from it. The imagery in the *Canto general* shows that it is for ever present, but infinitely preferable as a meaningful death in nature to the death and anguish of living social misery. In the following extract the natural, social, and historical planes of meaning are effectively contrasted:

> Piojos del mar, comed ahora estiércol,
> acechad los despojos, los zapatos
> rotos del navegante, del gerente,
> oled a deyecciones y a pescado.
> Ya entrasteis en el círculo
> de donde no saldréis sino a morir.
> No a la muerte del mar, con agua y luna,
> sino a los desquiciados agujeros

---

[1] P.N., *Viajes*, p. 18. See also ii. 14.
[2] Loyola, op. cit., pp. 31–41.

de la necrología ...
. . . .
hoy estáis muertos para siempre: hundidos
en el decreto tétrico del fraile ...
(i. 668)

Here the death of social injustice is a movement away from nature, from the death of the sea. Man came out of the sea to construct his organized existence on the land, and it is back to the sea that he returns in the most absolute sense. The sea therefore represents both life and death in relation to man. The sea has accumulated in its substance all the layers of time, and given eternity a definite form or shape. Eternity becomes for man something endowed with a meaning in relation to his existence. The flow of time is no longer outside man, who contemplates its movement with impotence and despair. Hence the precision and sharpness of the imagery in the *Canto general*, and the detailed structure of natural forces, which are catalogued in relation to man's natural, social, and historical existence. The sea's constant action on the coast is the wasting process of time which governs and shapes men's action, both socially and historically, on the land mass. Neruda addresses the sea as

> Tiempo, tal vez, o copa acumulada
> de todo movimiento, unidad pura
> que no selló la muerte, verde víscera
> de la totalidad abrasadora.[1]
>
> (i. 654)

Note the finite image used to denote time, *copa acumulada*. This gives the sea a definite shape in the mind of the poet and in relation to man in the cosmology of the *Canto general*. *Copa* is a major image in the poem as a whole, and one which is used to define the shape and substance of man in the opening poem of the *Canto general* (i. 319–20). *Copa* also plays a double role as the head or

---

[1] Note also how the conflicts of history become accumulated time in the ocean:

. . . . .
trescientos años enterraron
como la boca del océano
techos y huesos, armaduras,
torres y títulos dorados.
(i. 395)

top of a tree, i.e. *copa de árbol*, which links up with another important area of reference, the tree of *pueblo* as described in the opening lines of *Los libertadores* (i. 378). This image shows, therefore, just how the function of the sea is integrated into the social and historical levels of reference of the poem which are examined further on. Here, however, it serves to point out the central role which the sea plays in the natural level of reference as a key element in the conflicting forces of life and death which relate to earlier themes of Neruda's poetry.

From the very quality that it always possessed, namely the silence and stillness of death, emerges the language of life, for in his birth man begins to step towards death. This death, however, is not final, since man leaves behind shapes and forms which survive his physical death in nature by virtue of his historical dimension. The waves of the ocean therefore throw up life and death, and the statues of Easter Island suggest this theme:

> Miradlas hoy, tocad esta materia, estos labios
> tienen el mismo idioma silencioso que duerme
> en nuestra muerte, y esta cicatriz arenosa,
> que el mar y el tiempo como lobos han lamido,
> eran parte de un rostro que no fue derribado,
> punto de un ser, racimo que derrotó cenizas.[1]

(i. 663)

In Poem XVIII of Section XIV, *El gran océano* (i. 681–2), the poet addresses the rocks of the coast as symbols of shapes that survive time's action, or which are shaped by time. But he contrasts the life of rocks with the life of the land, since they represent in a most naked and desolate manner the life and death struggles of temporal or social man:

> El rostro de las rocas destrozadas,
> que no conoce abejas, que no tiene
> más que la agricultura de las olas,

---

[1] This compares with a well-known sonnet by Quevedo: '... yo soy ceniza que sobró a la llama', *Antología poética*, 3rd edn. (Buenos Aires, 1952), p. 43. This image of a branch surviving the flames can be discerned in a poem about the tree (i. 378–80):

> . . . . .
> y una ceniza amenazante
> cubre su antigua majestad.

In *Sonata y destrucciones* (i. 190–1) *ceniza* also refers to death by fire, but Neruda resigns himself to the fact and does not find any way to overcome his sad personal condition.

THE NATURAL PLANE OF REFERENCE

> el rostro de las piedras que aceptaron
> la desolada espuma del combate
> en sus eternidades agrietadas. (i. 681)

Here the rocks are faces worn by the waves; shapes or unities which imply struggles on land, but which belong to another environment. *Agricultura* and *abeja*, both land images, are contrasted with *olas* and *espuma*. The continual movement of the sea contrasts with the eternal stillness of the rocks, both absolute opposites. This opposition can be continued and developed, e.g.: substance of land *v.* substance of water, solid *v.* liquid, shapes that can be touched and transformed by man *v.* shapes that cannot be transformed by man:

> Tenéis, rocas del mar, el victorioso
> color del tiempo, el material gastado
> por una eternidad en movimiento.
> (i. 682)

The wave embodies all the energy of life and death that is contained in the sea, and furthermore the sea is eternally throwing out energy and movement without in the least wasting its central life and substance.[1] The salt of the wave is both life-giving and corrosive, and to embrace the whole magnitude of the sea, to discover its meaning or its totality, would be to discover the very secret of life. The wave throws up an infinitesimal portion of the whole substance, and Neruda always describes the wave in two postures, first as it is curved and ready to break, and second as it crashes down with a fury of destructive energy and sound.[2] The wave indicates, however partially, the abundance and fertility of life as embodied by the whole of the sea. In a poem called *La ola* (i. 670) the wave as it comes up from the depths of the ocean is compared to the organization and permanence of a rose that comes out of the earth:

> La ola viene del fondo, con raíces
> hijas del firmamento sumergido.

---

[1] See i. 654–5:

> ... Tu energía
> parece resbalar sin ser gastada,
> parece regresar a su reposo.
> . . . . . .
> Toda tu fuerza vuelve a ser origen.

[2] See the last nineteen lines of *La ola* (i. 670); this is mentioned in an article by J. H. R. Polt, *R.H.M.* xxvii (1961), p. 26.

Su elástica invasión fue levantada
por la potencia pura del Océano:

. . . .

Viene como una flor desde la tierra
cuando avanzó con decidido aroma
hasta la magnitud de la magnolia,
pero esta flor del fondo que ha estallado
trae toda la luz que fue abolida,
trae todas las ramas que no ardieron
y todo el manantial de la blancura.[1]

(i. 670)

The wave which emanates from the depths of the sea can bring with it all the accumulated substances of life in its unity, all the aspects of life which elude man, all the enigmas and mysteries. The wave in its permanence and its perfect organization is akin to the organization and substance of the wall in *Alturas de Macchu-Picchu* (i. 341), which is also compared in its organization and permanence to a rose. All the matter that the sea acts upon, including man, returns to its depth, and the sea never wastes one drop of its volume or energy. For Neruda this idea is one which contrasts sadly with the disintegration and corrosion that man and objects seem to suffer at the hand of time. How can man relate to *océano*, how can he extract from this totality a condition for survival? The forces of nature which govern the life of man are all contained in the totality of the Ocean. As Polt says: '. . . para Neruda, autor de una nueva y heroica cosmología, el océano es cuna de la vida, fuerza elemental, partícipe en el conflicto eterno de los elementos; . . .'[2] This mingling of elements is carried out in the body and substance of men, who, although they live on and and give shape to their lives on soil, nevertheless contain within themselves the substance of *océano*, which is at the same time mortality and eternity, since they return to the sea to live on for ever as the sea does. The rocks of the ocean are compared to man because, although the sea (in the shape of *ola*) continually acts upon them, it never succeeds in wasting them away entirely. The rocks are shaped and moulded by time, but they are not removed. It is precisely the same with man, for he may die, but his death

---

[1] The movement of the wave compared to the movement or cycle of the flower contains social and historical references in connection with *árbol–pueblo* (i. 378–80). The *magnolia* is common to both passages.
[2] Op. cit., p. 23.

does not remove him or his achievements, which he shapes with his hands from the face of nature. As a technical device it shows how Neruda still continues to approach the most abstract and metaphysical concepts in terms that are totally physical and concrete, i.e. through natural shapes and objects like the rocks, which have a far wider and more structured meaning than in his previous poetry.[1] This perpetual cycle of nature is played out in the nature imagery, but it also asserts itself as a theme of historical continuity which reflects the deeper theme at present under discussion (see i. 378–80):

> De noche sueño que tú y yo somos dos plantas
> que se elevaron juntas, con raíces enredadas,
> y que tú conoces la tierra y la lluvia como mi boca,
> porque de tierra y de lluvia estamos hechos. A veces
> pienso que con la muerte dormiremos abajo,
> en la profundidad de los pies de la efigie, mirando
> el Océano que nos trajo a construir y a amar.
>
> (i. 664)

Here the work of man, his loves, and his death are all directly related to the movements of nature. This ideal state of affairs is not always the case, as later planes of reference will attempt to show. Here the poet effectively describes how man's work and constructions (i.e. the statues) are intimately related to his origins in nature, and the survival of the statue, discussed in the previous chapter, will introduce an element of survival in social and historical terms as well as in terms of nature. For, as stated earlier, the statues on Easter Island and the walls of Machu-Picchu have a permanence and a structure attributable only to man, and they can be logically compared to nature, in that they survive the action of time like the rocks that win through over the action of the waves. In both cases it is interesting to note, therefore, that the survival of the statues and of Machu-Picchu are presented in terms of objects of stone enduring the action of the sea waves (i. 339; i. 662–3).

The existence of man in his social context on the land mass comes after his origins in *océano*, which contains in its waters both

---

[1] See his own statement on the relationship between objects and man in 'Sobre una poesía sin pureza', ii.1040–1; this originally appeared in *Caballo verde para la poesía*, No. 1 (Oct. 1935). Neruda's ideas on the subject have become progressively broader-based in relation to man; see the Introduction to *Las piedras de Chile* (Buenos Aires, 1960), pp. 9–10; and ii. 345–6.

the substances of the land, i.e. metals, plants, etc., and obviously also those substances which belong to the sea.[1] Most of the *Canto general* is taken up with man's human or social activity, both now, i.e. at the time that the poem is being written, and in the past, or in history. This of necessity means that the action and events are acted against a natural framework of land imagery, but this should not mask the integral role which is attributed to the forces of nature as represented by *Tierra* and *Océano* in the *Canto general*. There is a revealing poem called *El hombre en la nave*, which illustrates the conflict as embodied in man, where his origins in the sea and his existence on earth are contrasted:

> ... el hombre cierra sus ojos, muerde un poco
> sus pasos, amenaza su corazón pequeño,
> y solloza y araña la noche con sus uñas,
> buscando tierra, haciéndose gusanos.
> Es tierra que las aguas no cubren y no matan.
> Es orgullo de arcilla que morirá en el cántaro,
> quebrándose, apartando las gotas que cantaron,
> amarrando a la tierra su indecisa costura.[2]
>
> (i. 679)

This death on earth is compared to the much bigger and more meaningful death in the sea; a death which has been inside man always, which he experienced when he was born, and to which he is returning. Therefore death in a historical sense must be set against this death in nature.[3] The present extract continues in this vein, illustrating points made above.

> No busques en el mar esta muerte, no esperes
> territorio, no guardes el puñado de polvo
> para integrarlo intacto y entregarlo a la tierra.

---

[1] The synthesis of land and sea is well brought out in Poem IX of *Alturas de Macchu-Picchu*, where the epithets employed to address the city combine both frames of reference (i. 343–4).

[2] Compare this with a similar description of death in i. 341; the city, the man, and the *vasija* are all compared:
> Cuando la mano de color de arcilla
> se convirtió en arcilla, ...
> quedó, ...
> la más alta vasija que contuvo el silencio;
> una vida de piedra después de tantas vidas.

[3] The 'death in history' is systematically worked out in the *árbol* image, discussed in the next chapter.

THE NATURAL PLANE OF REFERENCE

> Entrégalo a estos labios infinitos que cantan,
> dónalos a este coro de movimiento y mundo,
> destrúyete en la eterna maternidad del agua.
> (i. 679–80)

The ocean here compared to a female form (see Fig. 4) is a standard comparison in the *Canto general*. Both the sea and the land are evoked in terms of the female figure, sometimes as a mother and sometimes as a bride or woman. When the poet expresses a desire to be at one with the earth and the sea, he addresses them as a bride or a woman, at any rate in terms where the male is united with the female. However, there is just as much emphasis on the origins and birth of man into life,[1] hence the image of the mother either as the sea or the earth. Both land and sea are givers of life and extremely fruitful, but the added connotation of the ambivalent female figure is that of life and fertility in the shape of the bride, and that of man's origins and return to the earth and sea in the shape of the mother. Hence the ocean is addressed in *Los nacimientos* as a mother figure:

> Estrella de oleajes, agua madre,
> madre materia, médula invencible, . . .
> (i. 656)

This contrasts with the last section of *El gran océano*, where the sea or *la noche marina* is invoked as a woman in openly sexual terms:

> Yo, noche Océano, a tu forma abierta,
> a tu extensión que Aldebarán vigila,
> a la boca mojada de tu canto
> llegué con el amor que me construye.[2]
> (i. 690)

The vision of the sea as a whole and the poet's close and intimate connection with it are systematically compared to a woman throughout the poem. There is also the added suggestion that the female form is a ship's figure-head, a favourite object of the poet's and the subject of a poem in *El gran océano*[3] (i. 676–8). This poem closes

---

[1] See i. 368–9, where the earth is described as both a mother and a bride in the same image.

[2] See R. Silva Castro, *Pablo Neruda* (Santiago, 1964), p. 101; he has an interesting comment on this particular poem: '. . . el elogio de la noche marina, que no es sólo la falta de luz solar que cada veinticuatro horas cae sobre el océano, sino otra noche, algo de metafísico y de íntimo, por lo demás frecuente en el poeta.'

[3] See P.N., *Una casa en la arena* (Barcelona, 1966). This volume contains

the long sequence about the ocean and illustrates the central importance of the ocean in Nerudian cosmology as well as its everlasting mystery. The whole sequence began with a plea that the Ocean might yield to him a fraction of its essence or meaning:

> Si de tus dones y de tus destrucciones, Océano, a mis manos
> pudiera destinar una medida, una fruta, un fermento,
> escogería tu reposo distante, las líneas de tu acero,
> tu extensión vigilada por el aire y la noche, . . .
>
> (i. 654)

In the final poem of this important section the same question or desire is reiterated, but it is obvious that the poet has identified himself far more closely with the meaning and shape of the ocean. The lack of knowledge and the eternal mystery of the sea are not the fault of the Ocean, but of man, who continually neglects to return and refresh himself in his beginning and his eventual end: *la eterna maternidad del agua*:

> Quién eres? Noche de los mares, dime
> si tu escarpada cabellera cubre
> toda la soledad, si es infinito
> este espacio de sangre y de praderas.
>
> (i. 691)

The same poem continues a few lines further on to portray the prime function of the sea as the ruler of all metals and the visible sign of true unadorned love:

> . . . .
> dueña de todos los metales, rosa
> de la profundidad, rosa mojada
> por la intemperie del amor desnudo.
>
> (i. 691)

The eternal nature of the sea and its infinite essence are woven into the final lines of this poem, where the poet's individual existence is poured into the limitless repository of the sea, which overcomes the finality of the individual personal death:

> Pero entonces
> entraré en la ciudad con tantos ojos

a description of the various figure-heads in the poet's home; *La sirena* (see text) may be the one mentioned above. See ii. 743–4.

como los tuyos, y sostendré la vestidura
con que me visitaste, y que me toquen
hasta el agua total que no se mide:
pureza y destrucción contra toda la muerte,
distancia que no puede gastarse, música
para los que duermen y para los que despiertan.

(i. 692)

The end and the beginning are compared here to overcome the finality of death, since the individual death becomes part of eternity in the natural death in the sea, which is the origin as well as the end, and the sea receives its most detailed and personal treatment. For the poet, the sea is an important entity to define and describe, and in the imagery of the poem it represents the guiding principle in one set of associations which are opposed to *Hombre* ⇌ *Tierra*, described in the previous chapter (see Fig. 1).[1] These two substances, *Océano* and *Tierra*, are contrasted, but they complement one another in this total or integral view of man in relation to his natural environment.

Now it is necessary to consider the movement of man on land, both in relation to the environment of land, and also in relation to the sea. It is impossible to evaluate one without the other, and, once *Hombre* ⇌ *Tierra* has been explained, one can begin to survey Neruda's cosmology as a whole; in particular, his account of the creation of man, which, although it has its origin in the sea, receives its most obvious treatment on land. For it is on the land that *hombre* acts out his social life and leaves behind his buildings and achievements. The land mass and the natural environment with roots in its soil, the minerals inside the earth, and animals and birds that move along and above it: all these are touched and tinged by the hand of social and historical man. On the continent of America, *hombre* has created his history and his life, and therefore much of the imagery in the poem as a whole relates principally to *Hombre* ⇌ *Tierra*. It is important, however, to describe the manner in which sea imagery invades the life of man on the land. The opening section of the *Canto general* (i. 319–34) is a scheme of creation on the earth, and describes the pre-Columbian civilizations

[1] R. Silva Castro, op. cit., pp. 102–3, discusses the importance that the sea has always had in the poetry of P.N., especially since he has begun to live in Isla Negra on the coast of Chile: 'Cierta ansiedad metafísica, transparente en muchos de sus versos más recientes, coincide con visiones marítimas. El verso alude ahora con frecuencia al golpe de las olas en la playa; ...' (p. 103).

as they appeared to the poet before the arrival of the Spaniards. The themes of this section, as expressed in the imagery, speak of cultures that were close to their natural origins, and of all their activities harmoniously integrated.

There is, however, a reference to the conquest of these peoples by the Spaniards, who are pictured as invaders who break up this harmonious relationship between man and nature. The description is carried out in terms of the use or abuse of metals and precious stones which originate in the soil. These substances have powerful natural, social, and historical references in the *Canto general*. The social and human evil of the Spanish *conquista*, as described in *La lámpara en la tierra* (i. 319–34), is seen as a conflict and confusion of natural forces and substances which can be used for good or evil by men.

> Madre de los metales, te quemaron,
> te mordieron, te martirizaron,
> te corroyeron, te pudrieron
> más tarde, cuando los ídolos
> ya no pudieron defenderte.
>
> (i. 327)

The earth, made up of metals which it yields up to man, is defiled and corrupted by the hand of this same man. The evil which overtakes America is described in oceanic terms:

> . . . . . .
> agua desconocida, sol malvado,
> ola de cruel espuma,
> tiburón acechante, dentadura
> de las cordilleras antárticas, . . .
>
> (i. 327)

The imagery presents a picture of land and sea mingling in a moral and social confusion, bringing with it the oblivion and death of the sea. Contrast this with a similar use of *ola* and *tierra*, when the poet describes the collective social effort that created the permanence of Machu-Picchu, which survives the action of the waves (i. 344).[1] Furthermore, the shape of the waves, the mountain peaks, and the shark's teeth all mingle into a conceit which gives a reference to destruction and death. This contrasts with the positive

---

[1] 'Cordillera esencial, *techo marino*'; see also i. 339, '*Alto arrecife* de la aurora humana' (my italics).

and the permanent quality of Machu-Picchu, which is often addressed in a similar display of elements:

> Novia del mar, . . .
> Ramo de sal, . . .
> Dentadura nevada, . . .
> Ola de plata, dirección del tiempo.
>
> (i. 344)

Here is the same catalogue of sea images, listed in a positive sense which is no way conveys the destructive death references of the passage about metals in America.

This leads to an important conclusion about the landscape described in the *Canto general*. It is that the poet sometimes implies different social meanings with similar descriptions of a landscape. Earlier it was shown how the description of a landscape contains a beauty and a perfection which contrast with the social anguish and misery of the people who inhabit it. That is, the landscape contains a potentiality of evil or good within itself.

> Cómo podías, Colombia oral,
> saber que tus piedras descalzas
> ocultaban una tormenta
> de oro iracundo,
> cómo, patria
> de la esmeralda, ibas a ver
> que la alhaja de muerte y mar,
> el fulgor en su escalofrío,
> escalaría las gargantas
> de los dinastas invasores?
>
> (i. 329)

The contradictions of history and social conflicts will be played out, therefore, in the very descriptions of nature, which is handled or manhandled by its inhabitants. By nature is meant the resources and the fertility of the soil, the fruits of the earth, and the way in which these are denied to *pueblo* by a minority. Thus what begins to emerge is a picture of a landscape charged with meaning for the poet, which contains within it a perfection in relation to the imperfect behaviour of men in their social activity, and also a landscape which is imperfect because it is abused by man. This fact enables the poet to proceed from a natural plane of reference to a social one with consummate ease, a point well illustrated by the following passage:

> ... natural conditions are not just passively accepted. What is more they do not exist in their own right for they are a function of the techniques and way of life of the people who define and give them a meaning by developing them in a particular direction. Nature is not in itself contradictory. It can become so only in terms of some specific human activity which takes part in it; and the characteristics of the environment take on a different meaning according to the particular historical and technical form assumed in it by this or that type of activity.[1]

This point is of enormous importance when we consider the movement from the natural to the social plane, where the poet tries to demonstrate social conflict in terms of the natural environment. This is particularly clear with the role of minerals in the whole poem, as substances which originate in nature and, like men themselves, are perverted by social use and abuse. In social terms this can be seen in *Las flores de Punitaqui* (i. 607–20), where the dominant image of gold is treated at all levels of reference: the natural, social, and historical, and in its individual meaning to the poet. As a result, when evaluating the meaning of the description of the land and its elements, such as plants, creatures, birds, trees, metals, etc., it is important to point out how the social and political elements have their basis in the profound theme of the conflict of natural forces within which man attempts to create a life or meaningful culture. It is wrong to view the political commitment as an unhealthy grafting on to the main tree. The social plane of reference is connected to all the themes we have been discussing. Many descriptions of nature contain, within their framework, social and historical references which the poet obviously intends the reader to pick up. For him the picture would be incomplete if it did not include the social reference, which most critics choose to discard. The description of the natural landscape before man, catalogued in great detail (i. 319–34), foreshadows some of the future agonies which the *hombre* of the poem will have to endure. In Section III of *La lámpara en la tierra* (i. 323–5) there is a memorable catalogue and description of some American birds. But implicit in this description of the beauties and perfections of

[1] L.S., op. cit., pp. 94–5.

natural creatures are the familiar images of social man. For example, the comparison between the dawn of the life of the Aztecs and the *cardenal*:

> Como gotas de sangre y plumas
> los cardenales desangraban
> el amanecer de Anáhuac.
>
> (i. 323)

Although, seemingly, this whole description is of an ideal state of nature, the description mobilizes the elements as a formal schema which refers to inescapable social events. Here the plain of Anáhuac where the Aztec empire held sway is referred to through the red chest of the *cardenal*, whose religious connotations make the poet think of the notorious sacrifices to the Aztec deity which regularly took place.[1] Hence the clever use of sun in *amanecer* and the reference to *sangre* and to the *plumas* which the officiating priests usually wore. *Amanecer* refers to the dawn of life on the earth, and it illustrates how, even at the beginning of man's history, i.e. his dawn, the social forms that he created were alienating him from a meaningful and integral existence in nature. The comparison between the bird's red breast and the colour of the dawn is doubly ironic. From a natural comparison, where the red of the bird's chest is so bright that it makes the 'rosy dawn' pale, the reference inescapably leads to the ripping open of the victim's chest with the obsidian knife and the extracting of the heart by the Aztec priest, i.e. *cardenal*. The meanings of *desangrar* are here cleverly employed, first as the *cardenal* makes the dawn pale, i.e. lose redness, because the redness of his own chest extracts the red from the dawn; and then, by a more violent historical and social reference, as the victim bleeds to death on top of the Aztec pyramid in Anáhuac. Hence the drops of blood to which the birds are compared (blood, i.e. redness from the dawn) become the bleeding to death of man by the hand of the religious oligarchy which ruled the lives of the Aztec people. In the same poem Neruda foreshadows the thirst for gold which will dominate the life of the continent, in his description of the parrots:

> Los ilustres loros llenaban
> la profundidad del follaje

---

[1] It also foreshadows the Catholic Church by the use of red, i.e. *cardenal*, the robes of a Cardinal. The Aztec priest is seen as the forerunner of the Catholic priest.

> como lingotes de oro verde
> recién salidos de la pasta ...
>
> (i. 323)

Here the green and yellow colours of the parrot are mingled in a stunning image, and his eyes become *una argolla amarilla*,[1] which forecasts the use of gold and all metals as jewellery, i.e. bracelets of gold. In other words, the picture of nature is not as simple as might be supposed, for it contains the ambiguities and conflicts of man's social activities, as the poet continues to list them in this section. The list of birds includes a veiled reference to the priesthood of Spain, in the description of the eagle (*fraile solitario del cielo*) flying high above the earth. This is neatly balanced by a previous reference to the very depths of the earth in *Algunas bestias*:

> y en el fondo del agua magna,
> como el círculo de la tierra,
> está la gigante anaconda
> cubierta de barros rituales,
> devoradora y religiosa.
>
> (i. 323)

The schema of nature which Neruda is listing in this section of the poem constitutes the beginning of man's life on earth, but it contains both life and death, both constructive and destructive forces. Here it might not be too fanciful to discern in this ideal state of nature ruined by the snake, a cunning Biblical reference, which would, of course, imply Christianity and the arrival of the Spaniards, the last contained in the very forces of nature, as the reference shows. The intention is not so much directed against the Spaniards but is rather a depiction of the social ills of religious belief, which leads to the domination of *pueblo* by a priest oligarchy.[2] The list of birds does contain some positive human virtues, as the rest of the catalogue illustrates. The *hornero* constructs his habitat out of mud and twigs, thereby exemplifying the constructive transformation and use of the natural for man's benefit. The list continues with the *torcaza* building a nest and multiplying fruitfully; then the *loica*

---

[1] The emptiness of gold jewellery is again referred to in the next section:
> No pude asir sino un racimo de rostros o de máscaras
> precipitadas, como anillos de oro vacío, ...
>
> (i. 337)

[2] The negative qualities of the snake are later invested with an evil social reference: see *La Anaconda Copper Mining Co.* i. 490–2.

THE NATURAL PLANE OF REFERENCE

is described as a *dulce carpintera del otoño*. The busy industry of those birds who construct and achieve contrasts with the negative social activities of the priest oligarchies which frustrate the potential use of nature's resources and perfections.

Therefore, the apparently blissful description of the landscape before man arrives has not such simple implications as might appear on the surface. The conflict of life and death contained in the imagery of the sea is carried through to the existence of *hombre* on dry land, and renders his life complex and ambiguous. The description of the pinnacles of achievement in pre-Columbian America is honestly re-created. The Aztec empire, its priestly caste, and the suffering people who built temples and pyramids for them, are carefully related to the earlier image of the cardinals and the dawn of Anáhuac:

> Como faisanes deslumbrantes
> descendían los sacerdotes
> de las escaleras aztecas.
> Los escalones triangulares
> sostenían el innumerable
> relámpago de las vestiduras.
> Y la pirámide augusta,
> piedra y piedra, agonía y aire,
> en su estructura dominadora
> guardaba como una almendra
> un corazón sacrificado.
>
> (i. 331)

Here the priests as birds assume the more elaborate form of the pheasant, a bird of vivid plumes and colours, its feathers rather like the ones the priests usually wore.[1] The pyramid and its construction foreshadow the structure of Machu-Picchu, which holds within its stone the agonies of the men who built it (i. 335-48). Here a similar development is traced from the symmetry and proportion of the stone to the agony and effort of the builders, to the heart of the sacrificial victim within the stone. This double-edged picture of pre-Columbian man is extremely important, because it leads us straight towards a crucial question about the origin of

[1] Neruda may here be referring to the *quetzal*, a bird of great beauty and stunning plumage, which furnished feathers for the priests and the nobility. See G. C. Vaillant, *Aztecs of Mexico* (London, 1965), pp. 176-213. These two chapters ('Religion', 'Ritual') describe the place of religion and religious worship in Aztec society. For feathers and featherwork see pp. 124, 147, 153-4, 234.

hombre in the *Canto general*, and whether or not the *Canto general* attempts to depict him as living in an ideal age before the Spanish conquest. The finer points of this topic belong more appropriately to the historical level of meaning in the poem. But it is important to understand that the historical references in the *Canto general* are to an order of events that masks a more significant structural order, related to man's proximity to and distance from nature, and by implication to a proximity to and distance from his own origins, which is referred to in the imagery.

What exactly are the origins of man in the *Canto general*, and did he ever exist in an ideal state of nature, as it were? One of the basic tenets in the whole poem is represented by the definition of man as the sum of *Tierra* and *Océano* (Figs. 1, 3) and both *La lámpara en la tierra* (i. 319–34) and *El gran océano* (i. 654–92) show man as a figure who arises out of the many organisms of the earth and sea to build a society in this natural environment (see especially i. 330–4 and i. 659–60). Before life on earth there was the sea, the repository of all time and all life, and the poet describes the early age before the dawn of social man as a tremendous interplay of forces, with the emergence of primitive plants and other organisms. It is important to note that the forces of the sea created or shaped the land mass, and the continual action of the waves against the shore remains to remind man that the Ocean is perpetually attempting to cover the land he inhabits.

> Y tembló para siempre en las orillas
> la voz del mar, los tálamos del agua,
> la huracanada piel derribadora,
> la leche embravecida de la estrella.
>
> (i. 658)

The beginnings of the earth or the universe are never even considered in the poem. Creation, or the origin of land and sea, is described as a series of transformations which give rise to the divisions of earth and water, both of which contain the energy of life in varying forms. The existence of man and the appearance of a natural environment which he begins to inhabit are not always clearly separated. There is no reason why they should be, since the framework of nature exists as a whole in relation to the whole of man, and it is in relation to man's activities that land and ocean are described. In *La lámpara en la tierra* the sequence which describes the metals in the earth is preceded by a forewarning of the treatment that these metals will receive from man (i. 327–8). The natural and the social are in this respect difficult to separate. However, the natural picture is one which portrays these substances embedded in the earth and originating from lightning and the stars.

> La hulla brillaba de resplandores negros
> como el total reverso de la nieve,
> negro hielo enquistado en la secreta
> tormenta inmóvil de la tierra,
> cuando un fulgor de pájaro amarillo
> enterró las corrientes del azufre
> al pie de las glaciales cordilleras.
>
> (i. 328)

The flash of lightning creates the rivers of sulphur which mingle with black snow, i.e. coal, at the roots of the mountains. But the description of the earth and its origins never clearly specifies a beginning. The main characteristic is that everything begins to be catalogued, described, and named. Because of this it begins to have life in the vision of Neruda's poetic creation:

> A las tierras sin nombres y sin números
> bajaba el viento desde otros dominios, . . .
>
> (i. 320)

This recalls Neruda's own assessment of Ercilla's *La Araucana*, where he says: 'todo esto tuvo nombre, por fin . . . y por razón del verbo comenzó a vivir.'[1]

But the catalogue of trees, beasts, birds, rivers, minerals, and man as the sum of all creation, is preceded by an earlier movement of natural forces. However much this may recall the book of Genesis, with which there are undoubted parallels, it is not a divine image that the poet seeks in the creation of the world. There is a similar creation sequence in the opening poems of *El gran océano* (i. 656–8). Here again the movement from stars to metals suggests a natural explanation of the earth's origins, where tremendous explosions and fires were succeeded by the formation of layers of the earth's crust, and the division of the globe into land and sea. Neruda's account of the creation is quite traditional, in

[1] P.N., *Discursos* (op. cit.), p. 62.

that he makes references to the separation of the four elements of earth, air, fire, and water into their respective domains:[1]

> Cuando se trasmutaron las estrellas
> en tierra y en metal, cuando apagaron
> la energía y volcada fue la copa
> de auroras y carbones, sumergida
> la hoguera en sus moradas,
> el mar cayó como una gota ardiendo
> de distancia en distancia, de hora en hora:
> su fuego azul se convirtió en esfera, . . .[2]
>
> (i. 656)

This account of the origin of the world is far more remote in time than that in *La lámpara en la tierra*; moreover, the sea is seen as a force which shapes the land where man exists.

> . . . .
> creó la tierra y desató la espuma,
> dejó rastros de goma en sus ausencias,
> invadió con estatuas el abismo,
> y en sus orillas se fundó la sangre.
>
> (i. 656)

The sea is the original shaping force of nature in Nerudian cosmology; a body which has absorbed all the aspects of the universe, it retreats to uncover land and swallows up whole mountain ranges that remain for ever submerged. In fact every single land mass has its roots in the ocean, and it is only the peaks which show through. Hence the nature of the apostrophe that Neruda directs to the sea:

> Estrella de oleajes, agua madre,
> madre materia, médula invencible,
> trémula iglesia levantada en lodo:
>
> (i. 656)

---

[1] For a discussion on the creation of America, and the conventional European explanation which had to incorporate the new lands into the *orbis terrarum*, see E. O'Gorman, *The Invention of America* (Indiana, 1961), pp. 51–69. Neruda makes use of traditional creation sequences to show that America is part of the Universe defined by the ancients. This problem is beautifully illustrated by the opening chapters of J. Acosta, *Historia natural y moral de las Indias* [1591], ed. O'Gorman (Mexico, 1962), pp. 30–56.

[2] This is also the case when reference is made to copper inside the earth:

> . . . .
> las venas verdes de la estrella,
> los finales fosforescentes
> de los cometas enterrados.
>
> (i. 441)

THE NATURAL PLANE OF REFERENCE 75

The stars of the sky are now contained in the minerals of the sea and land, and the sky is reflected in the vastness of the ocean.[1] In the depths of the ocean and in the depths of the earth are the substances which have been fired into the earth and sea by the heavens. The creation in Neruda is therefore a configuration and a distinction of elements where an inchoate mass assumes form and shape so that it can be named and described. When it can be catalogued and classified it becomes a part of man's cultural existence. The fires of lightning and stars are cooled down by the sea, the sea divides the globe into land masses, but the sea retains more than any element the original forces that created the world. The stars that become *tierra y metal* are contained by the sea in *estrella de oleajes*; and the stars in the sky retain a form which indicates that they have surrendered their fire to the sea.

> Mientras que como lámparas letárgicas
> dormían las estrellas segregadas . . .
>
> (i. 656)

The sea moves and acts with the fire that it has acquired from the stars:

> . . . .
> el mar llenó de sal y mordeduras[2]
> su magnitud, pobló de llamaradas
> y movimientos la extensión del día, . . .
>
> (i. 656)

The sea by its actions creates life and therefore time, and as the organisms of life begin to be named further down in this section (*los abetos, la madrépora, cetáceo, amaranto*), time begins to grow. This movement is the same in *La lámpara en la tierra*, where the naming of plants and beasts is the beginning of their fertility, which makes time begin growing (i. 320).[3] The part that the ocean plays in constructing and shaping the natural world is compared throughout to the constructive efforts of man, and to the shape of man himself. The structure of the ocean is evoked in terms of

[1] See Polt, op. cit., p. 23.
[2] Note how the description of the sea refers inescapably to the social condition of man through *sal* and *mordeduras*. The 1968 *Obras completas* does not have this line, whereas the 1962 edition includes it. Here I cite the 1962 text, p. 614 (see above).
[3] Compare with the unanswered question about the expansion of time in *Galope muerto*; see i. 174.

iglesia and *catedral* which have been shaped by the forces of the ocean itself. In other words, no previous force exists to control the movement of the ocean. The sea is the skin which covers the globe (i. 655); and it is also addressed as:

> Tiempo, tal vez, o copa acumulada
> de todo movimiento, . . .   (i. 654)

The image of *copa* as a reference for the ocean is a link with the description of the shape of man in the *Canto general*. The shape of the ocean is like a vessel of water and accumulated time, just as man is a vessel made of earth, full of life and blood (i. 319). The comparison between the shape of man and the shape of the ocean is a crucial one, because the movement and substance of the ocean govern so much of man's existence. The relationship of *Hombre* ⇌ *Océano* (Fig. 3) is thoroughly explored, with the use of comparative shapes for ocean and man. Apart from *copa*, another image used is *estatua*, which links with the *estatua* of man's form and the forms that man shapes with his own hands. This relationship is explored in the poem called *Los constructores de estatuas* (i. 661–3), and is further continued in the elegy to a ship's figure-head, Poem XV of this same section (i. 676–8). The whole comparison *océano–estatua* is picked up again in the final poem *La noche marina* (i. 690–2), where the shape of *océano* is mingled with the shape of the poet. The word *estatua* is important because it contains all the distance and limitless expanse of the ocean, which is difficult to encompass, in a word which is useful for the poet to relate systematically with the shape of man and the shape of man's work. Hence this word *estatua* is a good example of the connection between the natural plane, the sea and man; the social plane, the work that man puts into the Easter Island statues, which survive until today (which gives it a further historical reference); and finally, and most important, the individual plane, where the shape of the sea and the shape of the poet become fused. In all these cases therefore *estatua*[1] refers back to *hombre* (i. 690–2). Furthermore, when the

---

[1] The use of Easter Island (*Rapa Nui*) and the stone statues (i. 660–4) is a reference to the theories that were circulating at this time about navigation between the American mainland and Polynesia. There is much relevant material in the work of Thor Heyerdahl, *American Indians in the Pacific* (London, 1952). See, for example, p. 756, where the author notes the relationship between *Tepito-te-Henúa* and *Cuzco*, both of which signify 'the navel of the earth' and 'the navel of the world' in their respective languages. 'Myths and Memories',

THE NATURAL PLANE OF REFERENCE 77

ocean is addressed in this form, as an *estatua*, as in this line, for example:

Tu estatua está extendida más allá de las olas (i. 655),

this leads to a whole set of natural, social, historical, and individual references, governed mainly by the key role that the sea has in shaping man's existence on dry land. The time of the ocean and the movement of the ocean are the governing natural forces in Neruda's cosmology. The movements of nature on land are usually more closely related to the social and historical planes of reference. Hence the relationship of the waves to the rocks, which has already been mentioned:

> Piedras del mar, centellas detenidas
> en el combate de la luz, campanas
> doradas por el óxido, filudas
> espadas de dolor, cúpulas rotas
> en cuyas cicatrices se construye
> la estatua desdentada de la tierra.
> (i. 682)

Here, the rock's achievement in surviving the action of the waves gives rise to a very intricate set of references in the description of a perfectly natural scene. The sea's active control over the passive shape of the rocks suggests this land–sea relationship in the origin of the earth and man. Furthermore, there is constant reference in the description of the rocks to pain and suffering. This pain and suffering refers to social and historical man, who nevertheless survives this continual erosion, as the rocks survive. This 'oceanic time' is the time which man longs to acquire, hence the cry of the poet:

> . . . . . .
> dadme la condición que desafía
> las arenas del páramo estrellado.
> (i. 682)

pp. 711–63, has many details relevant to the mythological background of the *Canto general* in general. See also pp. 349–424, on statues. Neruda actually mentions pre-Columbian man sailing between the islands and the mainland (i. 659–60). Cuzco is mentioned in the opening section (i. 332), and Tepito-te-Henúa:

Tepito-te-Henúa, ombligo del mar grande, . . . (i. 660).

For a reference to Machu-Picchu in similar terms see *Las vidas* . . . (*O Cruzeiro*, 1 May 1962), p. 35: 'Me sentí infinitamente pequeño en el centro de aquel ombligo de piedra, ombligo de un mundo deshabitado, . . .'.

Note, too, the orderly progression of shapes in this classic confrontation between land and sea: *piedras–centellas–campanas–espadas–cúpulas*, all finally recollected in *estatua desdentada de la tierra*. These shapes are contrasted too with absolute or corrosive forces, *mar–luz–óxido–dolor*. But out of this conflict comes a definite shape of construction, the *estatua desdentada de la tierra*. This inescapable set of references to human efforts to survive the wasting process of time is further catalogued in a reference to Pisagua, the camp in Chile where political prisoners were kept.[1] Here a purely partisan political reference is played out with a full display of the natural and historical panorama, already well established in our minds. It serves as a good example of the fact that the overtly social content in the *Canto general* hides or masks a genuinely complex and ambiguous set of themes, which are directly related to the social comment by Neruda's use of images that have more than one level of reference:

> . . . .
> y en las desnudas grietas ofendidas
> está la historia como un monumento
> golpeado por la espuma solitaria.
> Pisagua, en el vacío de tus cumbres,
> en la furiosa soledad, la fuerza
> de la verdad del hombre se levanta
> como un desnudo y noble monumento.
>
> (i. 672)

Here the history of the oppressed collectivity and the rightness of their cause survive like the rocks continually lashed by the foam of the wave. The rock becomes a *monumento* compared to man, who also constructs equally eternal shapes, like the city of Machu-Picchu; and like man's own collective resistance it is a common effort that defeats the forces of time and *espuma*.[2] A further illustration of this point is provided in the same poem, where the ports on the northern coast of Chile are addressed in terms of their produce, *salitre*, which is mined for the benefit of foreigners. Here the standard contrast of *salitre–tierra*, *sal–océano* (i. 673) mingles

---

[1] See Silva Castro, op. cit., p. 100. He also speaks in this reference about the statues or '*mohais* labrados en la piedra de lava volcánica . . .'.

[2] There is an important relationship therefore between natural forms and social forms, brought about through words such as *estatua, forma, orden, sistema*, and *unidad*. This will be examined in the next chapter.

references of life and death in a natural and social sense. *Salitre* is *sal* to the Chilean and *oro*, i.e. profit, to the foreign exploiter. Thus natural, social, and historical references are all interwoven in this integral description of a natural setting which is so common in the *Canto general*.

The sea remains to remind man of the beginnings of the world, as envisaged in the two creation sequences in the *Canto general* that we have been discussing (i. 319–34; i. 654–92). The sea points to and reflects the sky and outer universe, it is the substance which cooled the globe into shape; and receding here and flooding there the ocean created land masses:

> Lo que formó la oscuridad quebrada
> por la substancia fría del relámpago,
> Océano, en tu vida está viviendo.
> (i. 656)

The sea is the first construction in nature. It is a force that shapes and constructs other substances, but constructed itself;[1] and it continues to move and give out energy which is both life and death.

> Se construyó la catedral sin manos
> con golpes de marea innumerable,
> la sal se adelgazó como una aguja,
> se hizo lámina de agua incubadora, . . .
> (i. 657)

But the creation in the widest sense precedes in time any creation that man may bring about on land. Neruda visualizes the earth when it was rough and formless, and clothes it with forms and shapes before man. However, the main issue in the *Canto general* is what particular use man makes of this creation, and the descriptions of pre-Columbian cultures such as the Aztec and the Inca do not imply any perfection or Golden Age before the Spanish conquest. Earlier it was shown how Neruda foreshadows all the social forms which will be the cause of so much misery in pre-Columbian America, in the very description of the natural landscape in the opening poem of the *Canto general*. The description of the Aztecs

---

[1] See O. H. Green, *Spain and the Western Tradition* (Madison, Wis., 1964), ii, pp. 75–104. This chapter describes the three aspects of nature in traditional cosmology; the role of the sea might be classified as *natura naturans* or 'creating nature'.

alludes to the domination of the people by the priestly caste,[1] and the description of the Mayas includes a reference to their sacrifices of young women:

> Con olor de razas graneras
> se elevaban las estructuras
> del examen y de la muerte,
> y escrutabais en los cenotes,
> arrojándoles novias de oro,
> la permanencia de los gérmenes.
>
> (i. 331).

The Maya civilization is commonly thought to have progressed further than any other American culture in the development of astronomy and science;[2] but here the poet unequivocally compares these achievements to their sacrifice of human lives in the name of a religion, and the fear of death which the religious ideology hopes to placate. Neruda has actually described the strong impression that these sacred waterholes or *cenotes* made on him: 'En Yucatán no hay agua sino bajo la tierra, y ésta se resquebraja de pronto, produciendo unos pozos enormes y abruptos, cuyas laderas llenas de vegetación tropical dejan ver en el fondo un agua profundísima verde y cenital. Los mayas encontraron estas aberturas terrestres llamadas cenotes y las divinizaron con sus extraños ritos.'[3] There follows a description of how hundreds of girls decorated with flowers and gold would be thrown into these wells. The flowers and the crowns would float to the surface, whilst the victims would remain at the bottom held down by the gold chains.

Neruda, whilst enthralled by the ceremony and the elements of the ritual, is not fooled into revealing a truly American Golden Age before the Spanish arrived. Indeed he goes on to say in the same place, after he has described these customs, 'Pero yo, al entrar en esas soledades, no busqué el oro sino el grito de las doncellas ahogadas. Me parecía oír en los extraños gritos de los pájaros la ronca agonía de las vírgenes, y en el veloz vuelo con que cruzaban la tenebrosa magnitud del agua inmemorial, me parecía ver las manos amarillas de las jóvenes muertas.'[4]

---

[1] Vaillant, op. cit., pp. 130, 192–3.
[2] H. C. Herring, *A History of Latin America* (London, 1955), p. 32. See also S. G. Morley, *The Ancient Maya* (Stanford, 1956), pp. 227, 424–41.
[3] P.N., *Viajes* (op. cit.), p. 73. Also ii. 44.
[4] Ibid., p. 74; ii. 44.

This is precisely the same movement as when the Aztecs are described: the priests and their feathers hide the innumerable victims of the sacrifices; the imposing architecture of their pyramids gives way to the stone that was fashioned by the men who died in its construction (i. 331). It is the same in *Alturas de Macchu-Picchu* (i. 335–48), which asks the question far more universally, and perhaps more regrettably for the poet. Having asked the stone of Machu-Picchu to give up its secrets, to communicate a language to the poet, he asks, in Section X (i. 345–6),

> Macchu Picchu, pusiste
> piedras en la piedra, y en la base, harapo?
> Carbón sobre carbón, y en el fondo la lágrima?
>
> (i. 345)

This questioning continues until the poet asks the whole of America, the whole of the submerged past, in the familiar form of address,

> Antigua América, novia sumergida,
> también tus dedos,
> al salir de la selva hacia el alto vacío de los dioses,
> bajo los estandartes nupciales de la luz y el decoro,
> mezclándose al trueno de los tambores y de las lanzas,
> también, también tus dedos,
> los que la rosa abstracta y la línea del frío, los
> que el pecho sangriento del nuevo cereal trasladaron
> hasta la tela de materia radiante, hasta las duras cavidades,
> también, también, América enterrada, guardaste en lo más
>   bajo,
> en el amargo intestino, como un águila, el hambre?
>
> (i. 346)

This question answers all the uncertainties and ambiguities which the description of the landscape in *La lámpara en la tierra* implied (i. 319–34). Despite the achievements, both artistic and social, it would seem that the men of America are hungry and living out the daily death to the tomb. But this gives Neruda's natural framework a great virtue which it is not usually held to possess. This is the implication that man was never in an ideal state of nature on this continent of America.[1] For Neruda the reason is not obscure.

---

[1] Neruda does, however, use conventional images to express the fall of man (see especially i. 368; i. 675–6). This topic owes a lot more to conventional literary themes taken from classical mythology by way of Spanish literature. Polt,

When there are societies in which the benefits of labour are created and used for a few who rule the majority, this is because the majority are being led away from the true meaning and value of nature and their origins, to participate in activities which are perversions of a meaningful existence, in order to justify the social position of an Inca or an Aztec priest. Hence the death-in-life which arises is man-made, and the view of nature based on religious mythology is also man-made, because it is invented as ideology to explain the situation in which a priestly caste rule a majority that it has enslaved. The efforts of the people, however, survive in the pyramids and cities they have built with their own blood in a giant collective effort. This effort is more noble and more enduring than all the ritual and religion of the Maya, Aztec, and Inca civilizations. The work of *pueblo* becomes in fact a more positive and permanent rite than the religious rites of the priests. In every case it is this aspect that survives in the mind of the poet. Take for example the description of the Aztec civilization in *La lámpara en la tierra*, Section VI:

> En un trueno como un aullido
> caía la sangre por
> las escalinatas sagradas.
> Pero muchedumbres de pueblos
> tejían la fibra, guardaban
> el porvenir de las cosechas,
> trenzaban el fulgor de la pluma,
> convencían a la turquesa,
> y en enredaderas textiles
> expresaban la luz del mundo.
>
> (i. 331)

Here the poet prepares the way for the great chain of continuity of *pueblo* from pre-Columbian America to the mines of Chile in 1948 (i. 607–20). The great discovery in *Alturas de Macchu-Picchu* is that there is an unbroken chain of continuity (i. 347), that there exists a story stretching from the men who built Machu-Picchu to the men who dig in the copper mines, who are described later on

op. cit., p. 30, suggests this in connection with Góngora. Probably Neruda is using other pre-Columbian myths (see Heyerdahl, op. cit., pp. 711–63). The theme of the sea and the crossing of the sea to search for power and gold is a standard topic of the Golden Age myth, as it is treated in Góngora's *Soledades* (see R. O. Jones, 'The poetic unity of the *Soledades* of Góngora', *B.H.S.* xxxi (1954), pp. 189–204).

in the *Canto general*.[1] The vision of nature and its use lie within the *hombre* in the *Canto general*; the same environment can be either hostile or friendly to the men who inhabit it. Take for example the section *Minerales* in *La lámpara en la tierra* (i. 328): here the poet asks why the landscape did not rise up to smite the invader.[2] Similarly, in Section IX of *Los conquistadores* the poet exclaims:

> Maldita sea la espinosa
> corona de la zarza agreste
> que no saltó como un erizo
> a defender la cuna invadida.
>
> (i. 356)

The truth is that nature and man are not united, as they should be, in an ideal state, because man has perverted his natural inheritance by the construction of false social forms and religious ideologies.[3] This inability to resist is continually alluded to, as for example in *Elegía*, Poem XVI of *Los conquistadores*:

> Por qué llegaron las llaves radiantes
> hasta las manos del bandido? Levántate,
> materna Ocllo, descansa tu secreto
> en la fatiga larga de esta noche
> y echa en mis venas tu consejo.
>
> (i. 364)

This is because the worship of gods and the tyranny of social injustice have alienated man from the proper use of *Tierra* and its elements, and it is amongst the Indians of his homeland that the poet comes across a spirit of resistance and strength which is allied to a true and proper use of the landscape. Consequently,

---

[1] Neruda looks into the pre-Columbian past to draw lessons for the present, as Mexican post-revolutionary writers did with their own native cultures; this matter is discussed at length in an unpublished thesis by A. P. Hogg, 'The search for identity in post-revolutionary Mexican writing' (London, 1967), Ch. 3, pp. 211 ff.

[2]
> por qué el coro de los hostiles
> no defendió el tesoro?
>
> (i. 328).

[3] It is in this respect that Neruda and William Blake come together; the fall of man is due to social contradictions, and religion or ideology in general is invented to justify the priesthood. See *The Complete Writings of William Blake*, ed. G. Keynes (O.U.P., 1966), especially 'The Marriage of Heaven and Hell', p. 153.

Neruda's use of the elements of nature as part of a formal schema to convey various themes, from the highly personal to the collective experience of social action and history, is a much more complex one than naïvely creating a Golden Age after the creation of the world, where everything was perfect and man was pure and guiltless.[1] Neruda's great discovery was that the horrible daily death and its anguish exist everywhere and always, but that the causes lie in man's vision of himself and in his assessment of the world around him. The unending conflicts of the forces of land and sea relate to unending conflicts between groups of men on a social and historical plane, where reference on one level has repercussions on the related levels. For example, it was shown earlier how the opposition of rocks and the sea involves themes of conflict on a natural, social, and historical level of reference.[2] If one continues to think in terms of this structure, it can be shown that much of the passionate description in the *Canto general* derives from conflict, where one way of life for a people, which is defined as total and integral, is challenged or denied. On a historical level this can take the form of a forgotten heritage or language which is glimpsed and recovered from the past; on a social level it can be seen as the creation or destruction of a collective feeling. All this can be reduced to convenient dualisms or contradictions: Indians *v. conquistadores*, *libertadores* v. colonialists, *pueblo* v. *oligarquía*. The first group in each set corresponds with the others, and so does the second:

Indians	— *Conquistadores*
Libertadores	— Colonialists
Pueblo[3]	— Oligarchy

Now these opposites tell a story from the very beginnings to the present day.[4] They also mask the more complex and internal struggle of life and death as suggested by the land and sea images.

[1] For an example of this view, which he uses to criticize Neruda, see Monegal, op. cit., p. 238.
[2] L.S., op. cit., p. 170: 'A society which defines its segments in terms of high and low, sky and land, day and night, can incorporate social or moral attitudes, such as conciliation and aggression, peace and war, justicing and policing, good and bad, order and disorder, etc., into the same structure of opposition.'
[3] This column shows people who are united with their environment; this unity can be conveyed in the word *patria*.
[4] The poet's mission or vocation to recount this story is continually stressed (i. 319; i. 347–8).

When considering these ideas in the next chapter, it will be necessary to ask whether these structures made up of related pairs of opposites are as simple as they look, in content as well as form. The people who make up *conquistadores*, for example, become *libertadores* in later centuries. Again, *pueblo* is made up of people with the very same Spanish names as those used for *conquistadores*.[1] In other words, what is really described in the *Canto general* is an opposition based on attitudes of mind towards an environment and one's fellow men; it is not an attempt to depict pure racial conflict or continuity. The key issue to grasp is that the attitudes which defined the conflict are the same, whereas the people who make up the opposing groups have changed. The enemy is not a white man but a *conquistador*, nor is he a *mestizo* but a dictator. *Pueblo* may be the Indians or the miners in Chuquicamata; they are *pueblo* first, and Indians and white men second.

The following commentary serves to map out what can be termed Neruda's closest approximation to an ideal state of man and nature. The piece also illustrates the devices used to describe the concept of *patria* as a union of men in their collective aspect with the various elements of the landscape of *tierra*. These parts of the landscape acquire overtones which relate to *hombre* on many levels of reference, and the active concept of *patria* is an ideal which is rooted both in a particular type of social action, and in the consciousness that *hombre* has about his origins and what arguments he draws from nature. The qualities and attendant images to describe *patria* are of some importance when comparing this term to *pueblo*. It is important to define and understand the meaning of *patria* in terms of the images of *Tierra* (Fig. 1), because it is on the basis of these that the poet works towards the social and historical levels in his poetry. *Patria* embodies the most personal and the most general references in the poet's frame of reference: personal because it is founded on the roots of his own past in the landscape and geography of southern Chile, and general because it embodies the creation of an ideal synthesis of man and landscape based on his personal vision and experience. The most potent devices for this task are the images which existed long before the *Canto general*,[2]

---

[1] Here again we are faced with the singular importance of names as a particular set of classifications which imply more general categories.

[2] See Alonso, op. cit., pp. 204–339, where the recurring images of Neruda's poetry before the *Canto general* are examined.

and which are part of the poet's personal equipment: these are *árbol, lluvia, metal, raíz, viento*, etc., all of which are mobilized with far more discernible levels of meaning than they previously possessed, as this commentary illustrates. Once the *unidad* of *patria* is defined on a natural level, one is able to move on towards related social and historical planes which follow on from the basic set of relationships. The central role that the Araucanian Indians play in the *Canto general* is clearly defined in the structure of the poem. First, they are the Indians who inhabit Neruda's homeland; they originally occupied the landscape to which he attaches so much importance. Second, they are described in *La lámpara en la tierra* (i. 333–4) after the more advanced cultures, in terms which clearly indicate that they had more permanent and stronger qualities.[1] In fact, they are the only pre-Columbian group who are described in detail with reference to any landscape, without any ambiguous social overtones. In the closing lines of *La lámpara en la tierra* Neruda arrives at the bottom of America to find his people:

> En el fondo de América sin nombre
> estaba Arauco entre las aguas
> vertiginosas, apartado
> por todo el frío del planeta.
>
> (i. 333)

Here *fondo* is both the bottom and the core of America; the other cultures have given way to these people, who will reveal the spirit of resistance as it survives in the forms of nature. The description of the men in Poem VI, *Los hombres* (i. 330–4), therefore, is climaxed with *en el fondo de América*; just as the description of the beasts in Poem II (i. 323) is climaxed by the serpent, also in the depths of the water. The positive qualities that the Araucanians possess are continually linked to the background or landscape. For this reason a description of nature hints at and refers to social and historical events, be they good or evil.

In *Vienen los pájaros* (i. 323–5) the Aztecs are referred to in the *cardenal* image (323); and the Andean cultures are described by the *cóndor* image (324). But the birds of the South, as has already been shown, reveal more positive qualities of life, work, and indus-

---

[1] This aspect of the *araucano* is also noted by J. Marcenac, *Pablo Neruda* (Seghers, 1963), pp. 19–37. This chapter ('Les pères de pierre') deals with the key role of these people in Neruda's poetry.

try. In the *Canto general* there is always this perfect movement down the American continent from the top to the bottom, always ending in the south, which is the Nerudian landscape of his childhood and the habitat of the Araucanians. This is the case in Poem IV, *Los ríos acuden* (i. 325–7), where the description of the continent as a female form works in a manner opposite to that of the standard poetic comparison; instead of using the shape of a continent to describe a woman, he uses a woman to describe the geography of the continent's rivers. The head-to-foot description of the woman parallels the head-to-foot, or north-to-south, description of the rivers, Orinoco, Amazonas, Tequendama, and Bío-Bío in southern Chile, which is at the foot and at the core of the poet's vision of man on all levels of reference (see i. 327). It is the same story with Poem VI, *Los hombres* (i. 330–4): here Neruda moves southwards, starting from the Caribes, to the Tarahumara in Mexico, down past the Aztecs and the Mayas, past the Incas and the Guaraní, to Arauco. In this region the various strands meet in the poet's vision of his own ancestors; here he works backwards from man to nature. The movement in the preceding lines of *La lámpara en la tierra* has been from nature to man (*vegetaciones, bestias, pájaros, ríos, minerales, hombres*). Now the poet contemplates the scenery itself:

> Todo es silencio de agua y viento.
> Pero en las hojas mira el guerrero.
> Entre los alerces un grito.
> Unos ojos de tigre en medio
> de las alturas de la nieve.
>
> (i. 333)

The Araucanian culture is described in terms of the essential features of the landscape; it is a culture prepared to resist and fight to preserve its identity. The poem ends with a reduction of the men to the essential elements from whence they spring; the poet (i. 333–4) works back from man (*guerrero*) to bird (*diuca*)[1] to

---

[1] See W. H. Hudson, *Birds of La Plata* (2 vols., London, 1920). This book contains descriptions of the birds featured in the *Canto general*; see also J. D. Goodall, A. W. Johnson, and R. Philippi, *Las aves de Chile* (2 vols., Buenos Aires, 1946–51). Neruda is supposed to have used this book when writing the *Canto general*. See M. Aguirre, *Genio y figura de Pablo Neruda*, 2nd edn. (Buenos Aires, 1967). This book has much useful biographical information on Neruda; see pp. 7–15, 122–51, where his activities during the years that he was writing the *Canto general* are described. Another source is *Las vidas del poeta* . . . (op.

beast (*puma*) to vegetation (*árbol*), and finishes with mineral (*piedra*).

The elements will be used to recreate in the present the existence of these Indians as a historical event and a reality, but here the poet seems to suggest that they are slipping away, and only the landscape remains to tell the story. There is an atmosphere of expectancy and imminent disaster. The whole picture is denuded of people and gets progressively darker. This contrasts with the dawn of man's hopes in the initial phases of the creation (i. 323). The essential features of this landscape remain as the sole witness of an age which will fade away into the past and into forgetfulness. The abrupt transition to the heights of Machu-Picchu (i. 335-48) in the present (the poet visited the city in 1943) poses this paradox of trying to visualize or recall the past. Hence the importance of the vision in this fortress-city. In the following section (i. 349-77), entitled *Los conquistadores*, the story of the past begins, and as the Spanish invade nobody seems to offer any resistance. When the Spanish advance has been described in the approved geographical movement from north to south (i. 349-68), Neruda arrives once again at the irresistible strength and permanence of southern Chile and the Araucanian Indians. Here for the first time the earth actively resists, and man and earth join to create a unity or a form which is basic to the remainder of the poem. The passage chosen for analysis is *Se unen la tierra y el hombre*, Poem XX of *Los conquistadores* (i. 368-9). The length makes it particularly suitable for treating the movement of thought as it develops, and it is useful for illustrating the varying references of the recurring images of *patria*, which are treated singly and together, as the poem shows:

Se unen la tierra y el hombre

Araucanía, ramo de robles torrenciales,
oh Patria despiadada, amada oscura,
solitaria en tu reino lluvioso:

cit.), and a collection of essays, *Viajes* (op. cit.). M. Aguirre quotes on pp. 166-7 the books that Neruda used to write the *Canto general*: 'pregunté si tenían algún libro. Tenían uno solo y éste era el *Compendio de la historia de América* de Barros Arana. Justo lo que necesitaba' (p. 147). The poet himself quotes two books that he used in i. 636-7:

. . . traje dos libros
y una sección de espino recién cortada al árbol.
(Los libros: una geografía
y el Libro de las Aves de Chile.)

         eras sólo gargantas minerales,
         manos de frío, puños 5
         acostumbrados a cortar peñascos;
         eras, Patria, la paz de la dureza
         y tus hombros eran rumor,
         áspera aparición, viento bravío.
         No tuvieron mis padres araucanos 10
         cimeras de plumaje luminoso,
         no descansaron en flores nupciales,
         no hilaron oro para el sacerdote:
         eran piedra y árbol, raíces
         de los breñales sacudidos, 15
         hojas con forma de lanza,
         cabezas de metal guerrero.
         Padres, apenas levantasteis
         el oído al galope, apenas en la cima
         de los montes, cruzó el rayo 20
         de Araucanía.
         Se hicieron sombra los padres de piedra,
         se anudaron al bosque, a las tinieblas
         naturales, se hicieron luz de hielo,
         asperezas de tierras y de espinas, 25
         y así esperaron en las profundidades
         de la soledad indomable:
         uno era un árbol rojo que miraba,
         otro un fragmento de metal que oía,
         otro una ráfaga de viento y taladro, 30
         otro tenía el color del sendero.
         Patria, nave de nieve,
         follaje endurecido:
         allí naciste, cuando el hombre tuyo
         pidió a la tierra su estandarte 35
         y cuando tierra y aire y piedra y lluvia,
         hoja, raíz, perfume, aullido,
         cubrieron como un manto al hijo,
         lo amaron o lo defendieron.
         Así nació la patria unánime: 40
         la unidad antes del combate.
                              (i. 368–9)

In the formal address 'Araucanía' is an equivalent term for *Patria*. The former relates more closely to a geographical landscape with a people, whereas *patria* is a concept which arises out of a particular union between nature and man, which is developed and treated in these lines. Through a description of the landscape the poet moves to a formal abstraction, from a localized description to a relationship between this environment and its inhabitants, which has crucial implications for the general themes of the *Canto general*. Here we are presented with the origins and the birth of *patria*, a process and an event which are summarized in the two final lines (40 and 41). This process is also a search for the poet's personal ancestry or origins, a search for his own identity and history arising from these events. The personal level of reference relates, however, to the poet's incorporation into a general experience, where he describes the origins and history of a whole *pueblo*, as it is born in the collective resistance of the Araucanian Indians. The passage as a whole breaks down into four well-defined movements, each a stage in this over-all movement that brings about a synthesis between *Hombre* and *Tierra*. The first movement, lines 1 to 9, is the formal address of *patria* as a whole, and the description of the landscape as a whole with its general qualities. There are also the qualities of the men who inhabit the environment, but they are not openly referred to. In this opening movement all the elements that will be treated in detail singly, such as *árbol* and *minerales*, are introduced. The shape of human beings is alluded to by the familiar reference to the female figure that forms a comparison with the earth as a whole. This also develops other themes which are worked out further on in the poem.

The second movement, lines 10 to 21, is of enormous importance: here the Araucanian Indians are introduced as father figures and as a group which elaborated a culture of simplicity and attachment to nature, which accounts for their lack of ornamentation and religious ideology.[1] This obviously contrasts with the assessments that the poet makes of the other civilizations described in the *Canto general*. The images used here are not in any way developed, for they are used to express in a negative fashion what these men did *not do* or pursue. From line 14 onwards the poet describes what in contrast these men were, and the parts of the landscape (*piedra, árbol*) that are used to describe them are the same as those listed

[1] Compare this with the description of the young Mexicans:

> En Cholula los jóvenes visten
> su mejor tela, oro y plumajes,
> calzados para el festival
> interrogan al invasor. (i. 353)

in the opening movement. The appearance of the Spaniard is less a description of the enemy and more a picture of the reaction it provokes in the ranks of these Indians. Because of their closeness to the natural landscape and their consciousness of collective action in the face of an enemy, they have not abandoned or perverted the higher virtues that man can embody. This attitude of mind and this defence of their land establish a concept and a precedent which will live on in the history of America and in the forms and substances of nature. These associations increase the emotive power of the recurring images which are used throughout the *Canto general*. Words such as *oro*, *raíz*, *piedra*, when used about the present, stretch back into the past, into events such as these. Therefore it is the clash of opposed forms of life, one side with an integral vision of man and nature, and the other side with a negative approach which is described beneath the purely historical order of events. This enables one to understand better the way in which imagery denotes social conflict in the *Canto general*, and how this issue becomes an unending conflict between two forms: on the one hand, people who represent all the fullness of nature and the earth; and on the other, the oligarchy (or *conquistadores*) which represents living death and the breaking or parcelling up of this fullness of nature.[1] In other words the social conflict is expressed in images of natural order and disorder.

The third movement, lines 22 to 31, is a description of the manner in which these people take on the forms and the appearance of the landscape in order to resist the invader. Here it is evident that the poet wishes to imply that nature will resist an invader only when it can ally itself with inhabitants for whom their environment or natural conditions are not contradictory, as was the case with the Aztec civilization, for example. Perfection, therefore, is something which resides within man, and his view of nature and its forms will either be ordered or disordered, depending on the use he makes of its potentialities. This is, of course, in a direct

---

[1] This image of a body or unity broken up will be closely examined in the next chapter, but it is worth noting the following remark made by the poet when he was in hiding, wanted by the Chilean Government. Here he describes the social situation in terms of a broken body: 'Hay un viejo tema de la poesía popular que se repite en todos nuestros países. Se trata del "cuerpo repartido". El cantor popular supone que tiene sus pies en una parte, sus riñones en otra, y describe todo su organismo que, segun él, ha dejado repartido por campos y ciudades' (*Las vidas del poeta*, Ch. 9, p. 36; *O Cruzeiro*, 16 May 1962).

relationship to the social and religious forms which the ruling class evolves to justify an unjust treatment of the masses, which relates back to their relationship with the environment itself. Hence the sinister and ambiguous descriptions of nature which contain both good and evil. In this passage the sets of relationships are considered to be ideal, as the descriptions of the landscape and the men imply.

In the final movement, lines 32 to 41, *patria* is again addressed as a whole in familiar epithets such as *nave de nieve* (line 32), for example, a reference to the mingling of land and sea so common in descriptions of Chile as a whole. Here the poet foreshadows the name that Araucanía will assume one day, i.e. Chile. But the key concept which links the two together is *patria*. Here, the birth of *patria* implies more than the description of a geographical setting, or environment; the concept denotes a group of people who have an identity, a culture or way of life that comprises as a part of it this geographical setting and environment that they wish to preserve as an essential component of their daily existence. To be born, to live, and to die in this natural landscape is very different from a defeat by a group who deprive them of their geographical setting and environment, and hence of their very lives and purpose of existence, which becomes, as a result, a living death engendered by social causes (i. 667–8). Hence the continual use of a nature imagery to describe social themes; hence the detailed catalogue of natural phenomena throughout the *Canto general*, which exists to show the bountiful and fruitful beauty which can be enjoyed by man, but can also be denied to him by others. On the level of formal poetic description or on the level of biased political diatribe the imagery of the *Canto general* unites all aspects or levels of reference.

The whole movement of this piece is held together as a developing argument by the use of well-worn elements of the Nerudian landscape: *árbol, lluvia, metal, piedra, raíz*, all of which are formally synthesized in a neat summation schema[1] in this last movement (see lines 36 and 37). These categories, which have been addressed either singly or together, are summed up here, with *hombre*, to give *patria*. Finally, it should be noted that the argument is structured and carried out by the use of repetitions, and of prepositions which Neruda habitually uses. Although not relevant to a study of imagery, it is a common device in the *Canto general*,

[1] The origins and use of this device have already been discussed.

and can also be found in the poetry of *Residencia en la tierra*.[1] In these earlier poems Neruda employs a fundamental technique of naming and defining a mood with key phrases or words. The mood is addressed or defined in different but corresponding phrases. The paradigm which emerges could be set down as follows:

>   *Hay* ... (a certain situation)
>   *como* ... (description of situation or mood)
>   *como* ...   ,,   ,,   ,,

This technique of naming and addressing continues to be employed exhaustively in the *Canto general*, where the difference is that the poet addresses cities, historical figures, rivers, countries; in other words people, objects, or places which have an existence outside him (see i. 325; i. 343–4; i. 407–9). This subject cannot be taken any further, since it would be necessary to study these forms of address as part of an over-all framework of epic devices that are employed in the poem. In this particular context it is worth noting the manner in which these categories present the imagery or mobilize the argument; for example, the verb *eras* in lines 4 and 7 of the first movement. The position of tenses plays an important role in indicating the passage of time in the *Canto general*; or (as is the case here) in indicating the importance of images used to describe something in the past, present, or future. Here, for example, Araucanía is addressed and described, with the important emphasis in the formal address taken up by 'you were' (*eras*) repeated twice.

Looking at the first movement in more detail, we find the landscape addressed in several differing but related ways. Araucanía is the place, *patria* the concept that arises out of the connection between man and this landscape. The further development of this formal address leads the poet to personalize the shape of the landscape as *amada oscura* and *solitaria*. These two images relate to one of the main connections in the *Canto general*, that of *Cuerpo* ⇌ *Continente* (see Fig. 2). Here the parts of the woman become the parts of the landscape; thus the *cuerpo* of *patria* is examined as a whole and in its parts. The basic structure of this opening movement can be expressed: *Araucanía ... eras ... eras ...*, where the verb introduces the imagery describing the landscape in lines 4 and 7. The earth–woman image is effectively used here to underline

[1] i. 173 ff. and especially *Unidad* (i. 177), *Tiranía* (i. 185), *Arte poética* (i. 189).

the poet's close involvement with the natural environment, and also the coming together of man and land in sexual terms (this theme will be developed further on). The notion of *patria* is introduced in this poem for the first time in the *Canto general*, although the notion of *pueblo* and the collective resistance of a people to protect their existence has been foreshadowed in earlier lines (i. 331).[1] Up to this point the poet has described the creation in *La lámpara en la tierra* (i. 319-34), where he described the pre-Columbian era; and in *Alturas de Macchu-Picchu* (i. 335-48), where he perceived the historical event of pre-Columbian man as substance that lives on in the present. In *Los conquistadores* (i. 349-377) that past, as it unfolds up to the present, begins to be described, and the collective effort of the builders in Machu-Picchu and the armed resistance of a group of Indians in Chile become translated into a concept which survives throughout the remainder of the *Canto general*: this is represented by the word *patria*. In these opening lines the bleak rain forests described are windy, rainy, and thick with trees. It is the perpetual landscape so frequently described in Neruda's poetry. This landscape comes to mean his origins and the most personal part of his poetry. The description of this environment, both in terms of the elements that make it up and in terms of the qualities that it possesses, contains inescapable reference to the men who inhabit it, even though they are not mentioned in these opening lines. It is the landscape as a woman, a giver of life, and man whom she brings forth, that is described. Araucanía is a name which designates not only the place, but the people; therefore the *robles torrenciales* are described not only for their importance as a feature in the landscape, but also because *roble* is commonly used to describe a person or a thing of great strength and strong resistance.[2] This place has a quality of strength which greatly impresses the poet. Here men live very close to a land which is strong and durable, made up of elements which the poet continues to describe: *minerales, lluvioso, peñascos, viento*, all developed progressively in the following lines. The hardness and

---

[1]
>   Pero muchedumbres de pueblos
>   tejían la fibra, guardaban
>   el porvenir de las cosechas, . . .
>
>   (i. 331)

[2] See Real Academia Española, *Diccionario de la lengua española*, one of the definitions given under *roble*: 'persona o cosa fuerte, recia, de gran resistencia.'

strength are balanced by a peace and an awakening of voices and shapes, as yet not explicitly described, in lines 7–9. The murmur of natural sounds which becomes the sound of voices crying out will be intensified, till the shouts of the Indians and the wind get progressively sharper. All this reaches a climax in the final movement (lines 32–41). Here by contrast the description of the surroundings implies simple but effective tastes, based on the strength of nature and its proper use by the men who inhabit it. As the poet moves down the shape of the female figure: *garganta, mano, puño, hombros* (lines 4–8), he moves through the landscape and its implied qualities. The images used describe a landscape of hardness (*minerales; puños*) and aggression. But there is a peace founded on austerity and strength. The remoteness and bleak nature of this environment are alluded to by the use of *despiadada* and *solitaria*. Thus every image of importance is introduced in this opening description and address to *patria*: the tree, the land, the air, the wind, minerals, and stone. Here the natural landscape is described in relation to its function as a background and reflection of man's social activity and his origins in nature. The main movement of the images, as a list of epithets governed by the use of the verb *eras*, links back to the address to Araucanía as a whole, and the use of the *Cuerpo* ⇌ *Continente* (Fig. 2) connection enables the poet to move from Araucanía to America, which he also addresses as a female form (i. 325). The use of the *árbol* image in the opening line is important. The tree introduces as always the idea of the collectivity: it has parts which form an organized whole, just as individuals come together in an organized *pueblo*. Here the whole of Araucanía is conveyed by the shape of the tree, and the forest made up of trees being lashed by the wind suggests the woman's hair being splayed out by the wind in the rain.[1] When the Indians come together to resist the invader, the notion that the poet attempts to convey is that of the parts of a wood coming together; many trees, therefore, unite to form *bosque*, just as many men unite to form *pueblo* (see line 23). Here the poem presents a landscape before man, before *pueblo*, but one which foreshadows the human beings in form and substance in the very description. The essential

[1] This comparison has also been noted by C. Meléndez, 'Pablo Neruda en su extremo imperio', *R.H.M.* (Oct. 1936), pp. 1–32. On p. 24 Meléndez compares this image with some frescoes by Dr. Atl, the Mexican painter. This image occurs frequently in Neruda's poetry, where the parts of nature and the parts of the woman are enumerated comparatively: see i. 325–6; i. 690–2.

difference between *pueblo* and *patria*, as the following lines reveal, is that the former (*pueblo*) refers to the collectivity of man, whereas the latter (*patria*) comprises the whole range of elements both social and natural in a harmonious synthesis. Though the lines show *patria* as the joining up of *Hombre* and *Tierra* (Fig. 1), *patria* also implies an attitude of mind, a determination to preserve a heritage and an existence. Hence the reference to *puños*, *dureza*, *bravío*, in terms of the landscape–woman image. This first stanza confuses the natural and the social, where the richness and fertility of the woman with her strength and peace give an impression of a land untouched by conflict as yet, but ready to resist. The elements of nature contain within them a potentiality towards both violence and gentleness, for the natural noise of the wind and the murmur in lines 8 and 9 are developed into a very human *aullido* in the final movement (line 37). The mingling of man and nature to give *patria* is, of course, further developed in *hijo* (line 38), as *patria* arises from the sexual union of man and woman. *Patria* has the strength to overcome and transform the natural environment, but it must seek and obtain strength to preserve itself. Therefore the first movement addresses *patria* as a whole in related epithets, and concentrates directly on the aspects and qualities of the natural environment that imply human or social qualities.

In the second movement (lines 10–21) the poet further develops the theme that the inhabitants of this landscape reflect the environment in their lack of a religious ideology and any luxurious adornment. This is not because the poet thinks that artistic achievements are negative; it is rather because the more advanced and sophisticated cultures failed through their own fragmented social structure to produce any kind of organized resistance. Again, as in the first movement, the verb *eran* (line 14) governs the description of the Indians. More interesting, however, is the antithesis–thesis construction which Neruda uses in lines 10–14; i.e. they did not, they were not, they *were*

> No tuvieron
> no descansaron
> no hilaron
> *eran*

By this method the poet attaches enormous importance to the list that follows the verb; and the things that they were are the very

THE NATURAL PLANE OF REFERENCE

features of the landscape described, now used to denote qualities and attributes which these men possess.[1] The Araucanians are shown to possess the spirit of organized resistance, by contrast with other cultures which relaxed, worshipped false gods, and indulged in excessive luxury.[2] Here, lines 10 to 13, the poet uses images which will not be taken up in the remainder of the poem, nor were they introduced in the opening movement: *plumaje, flores, oro, sacerdote*; they are used to describe false forms of life, voluptuousness and idleness. In particular there is a stress on the servility of people to religious ideology in the shape of priests. The use of *oro* is worth mentioning; here it is used in a negative social sense. This does not mean that gold as a mineral cannot be used in a positive way. It is an example of a natural substance transformed by man and put to improper use.[3] The people are linked to the poet as they are referred to as *padres araucanos* (line 10). Here in a picture of a collectivity that inhabits a landscape the poet makes use of the same formal catalogue of elements on a personal level of reference, where the place and inhabitants described are his ancestors. This landscape provides the poet with a setting that becomes an idealized picture or description of social existence and resistance in order to survive. The people fight to preserve an existence which is meaningful, because it is close to the movement and matter of nature. This is clearly apparent in line 14, where the harsh elements of the landscape described in the first movement become elements of aggression and resistance; i.e. forms which are part of the lives of these Indians. *Piedra, árbol, raíz* are by now images with enormous associative fields. These fields of reference are here used to describe the *hombre* of Araucanía; not only are they part of *tierra*, but they are also substances which point to the origins of man on the land mass, and his inheritance of the positive and durable qualities of nature. *Piedra* is determination and hardness, and *árbol* indicates both a natural

---

[1] A similar construction can be discerned in i. 346: 'Cuando . . . no veo . . . no veo . . . veo . . . veo . . .'.

[2] This, as we have already noted, provides a rich literary theme to be examined in the whole of the *Canto general*, especially in relation to legends of a Golden Age ruined by man's lust for power and avarice. In this respect Neruda is probably influenced by the poetry of Góngora and Quevedo. See Polt, op. cit., p. 30.

[3] Contrast this with a positive reference in i. 335:
 más abajo, en el oro de la geología, . . .'

and a conceptual reference to the *árbol del pueblo* (see i. 378), to be taken up in line 23, as the *piedra* reference is developed in line 22. The harshness and the strength of the land are carried on in *raíces de los breñales sacudidos* (line 15), and the movement from nature to culture is perfectly expressed in *hojas* to *forma de lanza* to *cabezas de metal guerrero* (lines 16 and 17), where part of a tree becomes the head of one man, who together with other men makes up *pueblo* or *árbol*, which is made up of many leaves. Here the shapes of nature become transformed into instruments of war to resist the Spaniard. The spear which is developed through *hoja–forma de lanza–cabeza de metal guerrero* arises out of nature, because the environment resists the Spaniard, since it is part of the integral existence of these people. In line 18 the poet becomes even more personal as he addresses these men directly as his own fathers, and begins to describe that union with nature upon the arrival of the Spanish horses. The main image in this movement is the tree with its roots and leaves, as it becomes (*a*) the head or tip of spears (lines 16 and 17) made of *metal*, which introduce *minerales*, mentioned in the opening movement (line 4), but now transformed into *metal* for arms; and (*b*) the symbol of organized resistance, both through its quality of strength, i.e. *roble*, and also in its structural similarity in the poet's mind to the people coming together to form a tree, i.e. *pueblo*. This whole movement closes with a similar repetition of *apenas* (lines 18–19), which emphasizes both the speed of the Indian's reaction to the invader, and also his lack of the fear or amazement in the face of the Spaniard which the other cultures exhibited.[1]

In the third movement, lines 22 to 31, the man described as coming out of the landscape melts back into the shapes and substances of this setting. This is both a natural and a logical device for conveying the idea of a social unity akin to the unity and permanence of nature. This movement is conveyed by the repetition of *se* in lines 22 and 23, referring back to *padres* in line 18, also the subject in line 22. The action of these Indians is *hicieron* and *anudaron*, one verb indicating transformation, the other adding or

[1] The Mexican Indians had been so frightened by the horses that they imagined horse and rider to be one creature; but see i. 389–93 especially:

> Marchó de día acariciando
> los caballos de piel mojada
> que iban hundiéndose en su patria.
> Adivinó aquellos caballos.   (i. 391)

tying themselves to something else. The men become shadows and retreat into the wood, which continues the major image of *árbol*. Here the familiar landscape of forests in southern Chile is mobilized to express the idea of a number of individuals coming together to form an invincible social unit. This also illustrates the manner in which nature opens its arms to protect and defend the Indian, in contrast to the events described earlier in the *Canto general*. The Indians become *asperezas de tierras y de espinas*, qualities that were described in relation to the landscape in the opening movement. The catalogue of elements, *piedra, bosque* (lines 22 and 23), is the same as in line 14. Whereas in the earlier description their relationship to these substances had been stated in a general fashion, now the process is examined for each substance or part of the landscape. Their silence and immobility is conveyed by *sombra* and *piedra* (line 22), their collective strength by *bosque* (line 23), and their strength and harshness by *asperezas de tierras y de espinas*. This element of disguise and deception is emphasized by lines 26 and 27. A general point worth making here is how the vision of nature in the *Canto general* depends on what type of social activity is being carried on within it. From now on the Spaniards find this landscape utterly opposed to them, whereas the landscape is in perfect sympathy with the Araucanians. As a technique this is of enormous importance in the *Canto general* (i. 368).[1] The poet demonstrates the device of natural description tinged with social and historical references, because the event of the Indians' resistance will live on in the permanent description of this landscape and its features, *tierra, lluvia, raíz, árbol, piedra*. From line 28 to line 31 the poet describes individual after individual added to nature, to the landscape as a whole; one is a tree, another a path, another a fragment of metal, another a wind which screams through the wood like a circular saw (*taladro*, line 30). Each part or feature of the landscape is a man, the totality equals the landscape or *pueblo*, and the synthesis of the two gives us *patria*. Here the poet has the usual device for emphasis, *uno era . . . otro era . . . otro era . . . otro tenía* (lines 28–31); the verb *era*, being understood as governing lines 29 and 30, emphasizes the manner in which the men have become

[1] El aire chileno azotaba
marcando estrellas, derribando
codicias y caballerías.
(i. 368)

nature. Also, the poet mingles sight and sound in lines 28 and 29. The Indian waits, all his faculties alerted, for the invader, but there is a further reference in the image of the wind as it becomes translated into a human scream. The image of the tree and the metal is not just a standard image, with which the reader is by now familiar. Here the metal, the tree, and the scream of the wind are all synthesized in *taladro* (line 30). The circular saw usually employed to cut down the rain forests of southern Chile makes a high-pitched screaming noise, which reminds the poet of the wind screaming through the trees and the scream of human voices. This is a perfect development of an image throughout the poem; in line 9 we have a reference to the wind, and the description has already emphasized the setting as a windy and rainy climate; in line 8 the wind has been foreshadowed by *rumor*, and now in line 30 it becomes the voice of man himself. There is a further reference in the manner in which the circular saw, controlled by man, cuts down trees, i.e. other men. This foreshadows the ensuing conflict, and it shows how the sound of the human voice arises out of the sound of nature.[1] Therefore lines 28, 29, and 30 contain successively sight, sound, and speech, all faculties which man possesses and the poet mingles with his description of the landscape. These parts all go to make up *hombre* or *bosque*, the image of the collective unity of man. This description of the movement into the forest is also the climax of the union between man and the landscape, out of which will spring *hijo*, the son of this union, which is at the same time the concept of *patria*, and also refers to the men who inhabit the landscape giving birth to *patria* inside themselves.[2] By their actions they change their situation, and bring about the birth of *patria* in their consciousness.

In the final movement, lines 32 to 41, the poet resumes the formal address to *patria* as a whole made in the opening section; but in between man has emerged out of the landscape and its features, and then gone back into the landscape to re-establish his

[1] The same device was noted in i. 533; for another mention of the woods of southern Chile and the circular saw see *Infancia y poesía* which forms an introduction to *Obras completas*, i. 30–1.

[2] The earth (*tierra*) is referred to as a mother and a bride. It is a bride in the sense that it joins with man to form the unity of *patria*. It is a mother in the sense that it gives birth to *patria*, which survives into the future, and the long line of people who defend the integrity and body of *patria*, i.e. the sons of *tierra* who are *pueblo*. By this definition the poet is both a son and a lover in relation to the female image of the earth.

true origins in nature. Now he can address *patria* in terms of all the features that have been catalogued in the previous lines. The first epithet used to address *patria* as a whole expresses the standard contrast of land and sea, which the poet always uses when describing *patria*; and it enables him to relate outwards to the concept of Chile, which will be the modern transfiguration of Araucanía. The second epithet (line 33) refers to the form of nature or the leaves of *árbol* hardened into a reality which is more than a vague ideal. It is also a reference to the *hoja–lanza* connection made in line 16. Thus *follaje endurecido* is an over-all term for the resistance which these people offer, and the manner in which the spirit of resistance and collective effort becomes hardened into a reality which is physical,[1] i.e. the tips of the spears. Lines 35–41 are governed entirely by *allí naciste . . . cuando . . . y cuando . . .*, finished off by a reference to *patria* as a whole. This movement conveys where *patria* is born and the conditions under which this birth takes place. In other words, this particular event can only take place when certain initial conditions are fulfilled. These comprise, of course, the social activity of the inhabitants, hence the importance of the negative list in lines 10 to 13. *Patria* is born when man claims his true heritage from the environment. This is all played out in the imagery which expresses this key theme of the *Canto general*, that the birth of *patria* only comes about when the men who inhabit a landscape take on a particular attitude towards each other and towards their environment. They must unite their common individual existences into a whole which is larger than the sum of their own particular lives. This is also an attitude which has to be based on an appreciation of their environment unadorned by religious cults or social fears, which pervert the truly natural or social existence. The poet continues to address *patria* in these terms in lines 34 and 35, and in the following lines (36 and 37) he brings together the landscape and man in a summation schema which shows the man and the various formal features of the landscape coming together, and is compared to the sexual union of man and woman, out of which springs *patria* or *hijo*.[2] All this is perfectly consistent with the poet's usual frame of reference: the earth referred to as a female form is introduced in line 2, and the

[1] The same might be said of the wall in Machu-Picchu, which survives to convey the collective effort of the men who built it (i. 341).
[2] The *padres araucanos* unite with *tierra* to produce a son, i.e. *patria*.

Indians are referred to as *padres* in lines 10, 18, and 22. These fathers are the first in the long line of *libertadores* (i. 378–459) who will succeed one another and keep the ideals of resistance, collectivity, and *patria* alive, through the image of *árbol* introduced at the beginning of *Los libertadores* (i. 378–80). These men are also the poet's ancestors, and Neruda's constant communion with the landscape results in a social, historical, and personal event. The link with the landscape expresses the dualistic tension which is evident in the *Canto general,* where the poet expresses the synthesis of man and land at a given time in history; but also, above this movement, it is evident in the use of images that the poet is defining and describing himself and his own origins. Here the poet's search for his roots in the past uncovers a whole theme, dealt with more carefully at a later stage. The summation schema which the poet employs in lines 36 and 37 is a frequent device in the *Canto general,* and it testifies to Neruda's deliberate use of the parts of nature as formal elements that can be split up and regrouped in support of an over-all argument or theme.[1] The various meanings that have been referred to in the previous lines of the poem are all contained in this unity, which is now formally displayed. These meanings are all collected together: *tierra–aire–piedra–lluvia* (line 36), *hoja–raíz–perfume–aullido* (line 37). The order of these features is also worth mentioning; *tierra/aire* is followed by *piedra/lluvia,* two opposites which are similar, since stone is of the earth and rain of the sky or air. The synthesis of man and land to produce *patria* is of the widest reference to the poet. *Piedra* has been used to describe the very essence of these men in line 14, and in line 22 they are described as *padres de piedra,* bringing together the idea of origins and survival in nature. *Lluvia* is used in the poem to describe the attributes of the land-

---

[1]
>   . . . .
>   era un árbol que se enroscaba
>   o una tortuga que dormía
>   o un río que se deslizaba.
>   Pero árbol, tortuga, corriente
>   fueron la muerte vengadora,
>   fueron sistemas de la selva, . . .
>   (i. 436)
>
>   De ventisquero a lago, de lago a planta,
>   de planta a fuego, de fuego a humo:
>   todo lo que arde, canta, florece, baila y revive, . . .
>   (i. 632)

scape, and to suggest water, which is outside man, but becomes part of him (i. 663–4).[1] Hence stone and rain bring together earth and air, but more significantly they unite earth and water, a crucial opposition in the *Canto general*. This is related back to line 32, where *nave de nieve* mingles land and sea, or earth and water. Line 37 is also made up of related sets of images; *hoja* and *raíz* define in more detail some of the features of *patria*. These two images connect up with *árbol* and with weapons of resistance associated with *hoja*, in lines 16 and 33. Both *hoja* and *raíz* are substances connected with the earth, whereas *perfume* and *aullido* are images of smell and sound discerned in the landscape. The sound of the wind in the trees is compared to the sound emitted by a circular saw cutting through wood in line 30. All these sounds that are akin to a scream centre on the human voice which cries out from the depths of the forest, or which is heard as the first scream of the child or *patria* when it is born. These images which merge man and nature in the unity of *patria* are a covering for the child, compact of both beauty and gentleness, and the harshness and violence to resist the invader. This strength to resist becomes a condition for survival into the present.

[1] The significance of rain and water are well illustrated by a personal experience recounted by the poet in *La copa de sangre*, which also clarifies the meaning of *copa* in the *Canto general*. See *Obras completas*, ii. 1054–5 (see also a modified version in *Infancia y poesía*, i. 32–3): 'Entro en un patio, muy vestido de negro, tengo corbata de poeta, mis tíos están allí todos reunidos, son todos inmensos, debajo del árbol guitarras y cuchillos, cantos que rápidamente entrecorta el áspero vino. Y entonces abren la garganta de un cordero palpitante, y una copa abrasadora de sangre me llevan a la boca, entre disparos y cantos, y me siento agonizar como el cordero, y quiero llegar también a ser centauro, y pálido, indeciso perdido en medio de la desierta infancia, levanto y bebo la copa de sangre.' Compare with i. 320:

> tu aroma me trepó por las raíces
> hasta la copa que bebía hasta la más delgada
> palabra aún no nacida en mi boca.

The importance of water, as a part of man which carries death, is well brought out by the second part of this extract where the poet talks about his father's death and cremation. When it became necessary to move the urn, 'vimos bajar de él cantidades de agua, cantidades como interminables litros que caían de adentro de él, de su substancia' (ii. 1055). Neruda concludes: 'esta agua trágica era lluvia ... esta agua original y temible me advertía otra vez con su misterioso derrame mi conexión interminable con una determinada vida, región y muerte' (ii. 1055). *Copa de sangre* can be found also in *Poesías completas* (Buenos Aires, 1951), and in *Obra poética de P.N.* (Santiago, 1947–8), vol. 7, pp. 71–3. It is also quoted by Aguirre, op. cit., pp. 28–30, and Rodríguez Monegal, op. cit., pp. 31–2.

The final two lines sum up the whole movement of the poem; they also summarize this integral existence of a group of individuals who construct a culture that unifies all aspects of life and nature. This is the meaning of *unidad* and *patria* in lines 40 and 41; *patria* or the proper relationship of man to nature is a distinctly human achievement. There is nothing mystical or vague about these connections. The poet is at pains to emphasize throughout the *Canto general* that it is nature as it is viewed by man himself that is the most important factor in the description of the environment. What the poet has done is to abstract the various elements from the landscape and distribute them individually throughout the poem in relation to man, regrouping them with the added layers of reference in the summation schema at the end. The structure of the imagery refers in the one poem to the social qualities of the Indians manifested in their collective resistance to the invader. This also arises out of a particular natural setting which is formally linked to the activities of these people. Historically, the images refer to an event in history as it relates to present or contemporary events, by giving them a beginning in the past leading up to the present. The most important concept that arises out of this detailed analysis is the notion of *patria*, which is at the very centre of the *Canto general*. In this image the poet's emotional relationship to the landscape, his origins in the landscape, his relations to past events, and his place in a larger framework are all grouped together. This synthesis is the *unidad* referred to in line 41; it is also this integral quality which unites all levels of reference in the poem from the landscape to the individual person of the poet.[1] This *unidad* can now be compared to the unity of natural forms which man attains because of his positive social and cultural achievements.[2]

[1] See *Discursos*, p. 62.
[2] See i. 654:

>   Océano . . .
>   . . . unidad pura
>   que no selló la muerte, . . .

and p. 670:
>   La ola . . .
>   . . . es la unidad del mar que se construye: . . .

III

THE SOCIAL AND HISTORICAL PLANES OF REFERENCE

THE social and political references in the *Canto general* are the most important area of meaning to assess in relation to an over-all view of the poem. The structured images employed by the poet on the social level of reference are the same ones that he resorts to when writing about different but interconnected areas of meaning. It is important to regard political diatribe and descriptions of nature as inexorably interwoven with personal and collective historical references. And for this reason, too, the social content should not be regarded as in any way a debasement of Neruda's imagery. The matter should be considered as something which constitutes a growth or development in the themes of Neruda's poetry. Finally, when considering the images of the *Canto general*, the social themes should be viewed as contributing richer meanings and further associations which enlarge the poet's previous field of reference. The last chapter attempted to show this process at work in the ordered description of a landscape, or in the catalogue of birds, for example (i. 323–5).[1] Neruda's description of pre-Columbian man in the first two sections of the *Canto general* (i. 319–48) had inescapable social comment implicit in the arrangement and associations of the imagery. The most important theme, however, is the growth and the manifestation of a collective consciousness as exhibited by the Indians of Araucanía who resist the Spaniards. The images used to portray this spirit of resistance find their synthesis in concepts such as *pueblo* and *patria*. This last concept is the synthesis of *Hombre* and *Tierra* in a unity which is crucial to the social argument of the *Canto general*. *Patria* is the complete cultural system, incorporating land and plants, customs and utensils, which *pueblo* defend as their very own

---

[1] For an example of Neruda's interest in ornithology, and nature in general, see M. Rivero de la Calle, 'Pablo Neruda, poeta y naturalista', *Islas*, vol. 3, No. 3 (Cuba, May–Aug. 1961), pp. 99–106.

person, as if they were their own physical selves.[1] Hence the importance of systematic connections between *Hombre*⇌*Tierra*, described elsewhere. Man's cultural or social activity indicates that he is not in nature, but that he has a culture which makes him separate from nature, whilst he yet employs parts of nature to manufacture his culture. This lives on, apart from nature, as history which is the record of man's activities within a framework of nature. The questions that this chapter seeks to answer, therefore, are, first, how the existence of a social group is portrayed in the *Canto general* in terms of imagery, and second, in what manner the continual themes of conflict are played out in terms of opposing imagery. Finally, this chapter considers how these images, because of their systematic relationships and references which keep recurring throughout the poem, build up an effective network of historical reference within one unchanging structure.

The key issue to begin with, therefore, is that *patria* when inhabited and used by *pueblo* has all the images of order, harmony, fertility, unity, language, life, and light, and that it is continually threatened and opposed by *conquistadores*, landowners, imperialists, and oligarchies, who bring with them disorder, discord, sterility, disunity, silence, death, and darkness.[2] As a result of this opposition apparently superficial political passages betray a complex network of images continually shifting between order and disorder, unity and disunity, life and death, and so on. Throughout the poem the attendant images round *patria* and *pueblo* strive to communicate to the reader that this positive social action, in the shape of collective activity, is an awakening in the minds of the people; that the people are *pueblo* with a unity, a system, and an order which they can bring about through their own efforts. For this reason the poet, when describing a traditional American hero, such as San Martín, for example (i. 407–9), makes great use of words such as *cuerpo*, *geografía*, *estatura*. This point enables individual and social activity to be compared and contrasted with the activity and achievement of nature. For as nature shapes and creates, so does man, to a lesser or greater degree. Again, the example of Recabarren (i. 445–50), the Chilean labour leader, is instructive: here the poet clearly demonstrates a technique which is constant through the *Canto general*. This is his use of famous individuals in American history, such as Bolívar (i. 420–2) or Martí (i. 428–9)

[1] See P.N., *Discursos*, p. 62. [2] See Monguió, op. cit., p. 26.

or Recabarren, as people who represent *pueblo* and *patria*. By this it is meant that the poet does not describe them as heroic individuals in their own right, but as men who organized, ordered, or structured the hand and voice of *pueblo* in their own person. This relationship between individual and collectivity is of prime importance in the *Canto general*, as Rodríguez Monegal has noted:

En lugar de una sucesión de héroes patrióticos que cada oligarquía local esculpe en mármol o bronce para perpetuar a su sombra esos mismos beneficios y privilegios que los héroes trataron vanamente de destruir, ahora presenta Neruda la verdadera raíz del heroísmo americano, denuncia a los venales y vendepatrias y restaura a la masa anónima a su verdadero lugar de paciente histórico. Esa multitud indígena que vive secularmente al margen de la historia, . . . aparece plena y fuerte, a ratos heroica, en el *Canto general*. Es la misma masa que construye, piedra sobre piedra, esa enorme América pero nunca figura en la hora de las grandes recompensas.[1]

Pueblo is the real protagonist of the *Canto general*, and it is the collectivity as it manifests itself through traditional heroes that the poet describes. In *Los libertadores* Recabarren (i. 445–50) is introduced as an individual figure, and straight away related to the desert sand of northern Chile. In other words, the description of one man becomes the description of the landscape and its inhabitants. Furthermore, the initial description is one of destruction and disorder, where the people live in social poverty and confusion within a natural framework of mineral products that are rich and abundant. The fundamental *Body*⇌*Continent* relationship is here introduced, linking the description of the landscape with the description of Recabarren. In the opening lines the poet connected the numerous grains of sand with the body of the hero, and both were described as hiding or concealing strength and deposits of wealth. The grains of sand that are so numerous lead through to the many inhabitants of northern Chile, equally numerous and so poor, who will come to achieve strength through unity. All this is carried out in the structure and organization of the images. Thus Recabarren is described in relation to the soil and its resources:

. . . . . .
su ancha compostura cubría,

[1] op. cit., p. 239.

> como la arena numerosa,
> los yacimientos de la fuerza.
>
> (i. 445)

Here the mineral deposits which lie under the ground, concealed by the sand, are deposits of a strength, natural and social alike. The connection is carried on lower down, where the poet describes the metals and their strength, order, and wealth, but contrasts this with the weakness, disorder, and poverty of the individual.

> Sobre las áreas musculares
> de los metales y el nitrato,
> sobre la atlética grandeza
> del cobre recién excavado,
> el pequeño habitante vive,
> acumulado en el desorden,
> con un contrato apresurado,
> lleno de niños andrajosos,
> extendidos por los desiertos
> de la superficie salada. (i. 445)

The metals are muscular and athletic, the inhabitant is small, weak, and a body of social misery. The desert is for him a harsh place; but the movement of the poem will show the reader that this need not be the natural order of things. Clearly, there is here a situation where the order and unity of nature are not reflected in any comparable way by an order and unity of man. The description of a standard hero, of exalted stature, has led through to the description of the anonymous Chilean worker who is the true hero of the poem:

> Es el chileno interrumpido
> por la cesantía o la muerte.
>
> (i. 445)

From the disjointed description of the body of 'Chile con su destrozada biología', as the poet described it earlier, the poem moves through to a description of an emerging unity, order, and strength comparable to the minerals in the body of the earth. This process involves several important stages: first of all it is a matter of joining one individual to another into a strong body; it also is a question of constructing the strength and unity of *pueblo* with the hands of the people themselves. The next stage of the process involves the giving of voice, activity, and words to what was previously silent and passive. Most important of all, however, is the awakening in the minds of the people of a new relationship between themselves and their environment. They are to realize through the body of landscape and its attendant parts that they can employ these resources for their own social body and its parts. Thus, whenever there is a manifestation of *pueblo* in the *Canto general*, it springs like a natural growth from the soil itself, when the people renew their lost contact with the earth and its fruits and fashion their own salvation. This aspect, with its important features of a resumption or renewal of a past inheritance either lost or forgotten, is a key process in the *Canto general*, which will be studied further in the second part of this chapter. Thus, when Recabarren speaks and organizes, he gives speech and organization to everybody:

>«Junta tu voz a otra voz»,
>«Junta tu mano a otra mano.»
>Fue por los rincones aciagos
>del salitre, llenó la pampa
>con su investidura paterna
>y en el escondite invisible
>lo vió toda la minería.
>
>(i. 446)

The movement towards order and strength in a social sense is paralleled by a similar movement which brings together the minerals and man and gives the landscape a unity which previously had not existed, the *unidad* of *pueblo* and *patria*. *Unidad* on a natural plane can therefore be contrasted with a lack of unity on a social plane, and descriptions of nature, as previous chapters have shown, serve either to illustrate a social ideal when *pueblo* and *patria* are in harmony with nature, or to make an effective social point when *pueblo* and *patria* are poor and disunited, because the people are not benefiting from nature. The important point to bring out here is that the description of a landscape and its parts is mobilized in support of an argument, and viewed on one plane only, the landscape as a whole comes together to make an effective social point.

Hence the significance of the movement in the following verse, where the poet illustrates the transformation of the silent, passive individual into the vociferous, active unity of the collectivity, as a coming together of people and metals, culminating in a unity that relates the social and the natural:

> Y este habitante transformado
> que se construyó en el combate,
> este organismo valeroso,
> esta implacable tentativa,
> este metal inalterable,
> esta unidad de los dolores,
> esta fortaleza del hombre,
> este camino hacia mañana,
> esta cordillera infinita,
> esta germinal primavera,
> este armamento de los pobres, . . .
>
> (i. 447)

The movement towards a social unity has resulted in a comparable movement in all the areas of reference in the poetry. The poet moves between the body of man and the body of the collectivity, between the strength of man and the strength of *cordillera*, or between the unity of individuals and the unity of metals. The main issue is, however, the coming together of *pueblo* and *tierra* in a new and more enduring *unidad*. Therefore Neruda demonstrates for us yet again through the images and their reference the many levels of argument that a landscape can hold for his imagination. For it is in the *cordillera infinita* and the *germinal primavera* that the unity and organization of social and political concepts are summed up. This poem addressed to Recabarren continues to describe the permanence and organization of *pueblo* as 'luz organizada por las manos de Recabarren' or 'unidad del tiempo que amanece'. Here the poet relates images of light and unity to the person of the hero. Furthermore, the images combine a sense of natural order and harmony with a comparable man-made order and harmony. The natural and the social complement one another and achieve their maximum unity in movements of collective work, or resistance to the enemies of the collectivity. Recabarren is like all other heroes or *libertadores* in the *Canto general*, in that he is both a father and a son, as the following lines show:

> Recabarren, hijo de Chile,
> padre de Chile, padre nuestro,
> en tu construcción, en tu línea

> fraguada en tierras y tormentos
> nace la fuerza de los días
> venideros y vencedores.
>
> (i. 449–50)

Here the poet moves to close the formal invocation of Recabarren's achievements by stressing how the size and shape of his accomplishments are grouped together and expressed in the shape of his figure. As a hero he is a father, in that he brings about the birth of *pueblo* and future *libertadores*; but he is also a son, because he is but one stage in a long line of *libertadores* who arise out of the soil and the past of Chile to bring light and order in troubled times.[1] Heroes like Recabarren, therefore, represent firstly *pueblo*, because they give it an existence and a voice, and secondly *patria*, because they re-awake in the minds of the people the lost or forgotten consciousness of *patria*, which is the people's relationship with *tierra*.[2] This is neatly illustrated in a final definition of Recabarren before the poem closes, on a note of unity, order, life, fertility, and social activity. The elements enumerated are all correlated or gathered in the figure of Recabarren, at the beginning of the enumeration rather than in the final verses:

> Tú eres la patria, pampa y pueblo,
> arena, arcilla, escuela, casa,
> resurrección, puño, ofensiva,
> orden, desfile, ataque, trigo,
> lucha, grandeza, resistencia.   (i. 450)

The poet uses the same device as with San Martín (i. 407), for example the continued use of 'tú eres...', followed by a description of the landscape and attendant images of the order and fullness of nature. Here, as in the example of San Martín, man and land come together to illustrate the positive and enduring nature

---

[1] It is important to recall that in any relationship between *hombre* and *tierra* the earth is feminine. Thus Recabarren is both a father, when he fertilizes the earth-woman, and a son, when he comes out of the earth-mother.

[2] An important device is the use of phrases from the Lord's Prayer as a form of address. This reinforces the social meaning; the salvation of men lies not with God, but in the words and deeds of men like Recabarren. The earliest use of this form of address is in *Tercera residencia*, in a poem addressed to Bolívar:

> Padre nuestro que estás en la tierra, en el agua, en el aire...
>
> (i. 306)

of their achievements, both then and now in the present.[1] Natural substances are compared and contrasted with human dwellings constructed by man, and the flowering of wheat is related in a similar manner to the resurrection out of the earth of human hopes and strength. Therefore, in the recurring descriptions of nature and the apostrophe of traditional heroes in American history these images are displayed in formal patterns, to make an effective social point about *pueblo* and *patria* as a unity or body which continually survives to win in the end. This is particularly well illustrated in another apostrophe to a traditional hero, Tupac Amaru (1781) (i. 401-2). Here the Indian leader observes the mingling of social torment and the natural cycle bursting forth:[2]

> viste subir a Tungasuca
> la primavera desolada
> de los escalones andinos,
> y con ella sal y desdicha,
> iniquidades y tormentos.
>
> (i. 401)

The role of the hero is to divine the magnitude of the suffering of each individual and to bring them all together. The hero or *libertador* also perceives the past sufferings of *pueblo* and brings these out of oblivion, giving them a voice as well:[3]

> El indio te mostró la espalda
> en que las nuevas mordeduras
> brillaban en las cicatrices
> de otros castigos apagados,

[1] Y así eres, hasta hoy, luna y galope,
estación de soldados, intemperie,
por donde vamos otra vez guerreando,
caminando entre pueblos y llanuras, ...
(i. 408)

[2] Tungasuca was the region where Tupac Amaru was born. He inherited the title of *curaca* of Tungasuca and Sicuani on the death of his father, Miguel Condorcanqui. This area is in the Wilkamayu valley, not far from Cuzco. The area is both rich in vegetation and steeply mountainous. See P. A. Means, 'The rebellion of Tupac Amaru', *H.A.H.R.* ii (1919), pp. 1-25.

[3] See the final lines of *Alturas de Macchu-Picchu* (i. 347):

> Mostradme vuestra sangre y vuestro surco,
> decidme: aquí fui castigado, ...
> . . . . . .
> encendedme los viejos pedernales,
> las viejas lámparas, los látigos pegados
> a través de los siglos en las llagas ...

Neruda as the present *libertador* perceives the past sufferings as well.

THE SOCIAL AND HISTORICAL PLANES

> y era una espalda y otra espalda,
> toda la altura sacudida
> por las cascadas del sollozo. (i. 401)

The Indian leader brings together wounds, backs, and cries, lending a voice to hitherto individual sufferings in the shape of a collective cry. The unification of all these individual tears in one form is represented by the use of the word *copa*. Tupac Amaru gathers in his cup or shape the waterfall of tears. *Copa*[1] is frequently the empty vessel or shape of a man which can be filled by various liquids. Here the reference is two-fold: first all the cries of *pueblo* come together in the shape of the hero's *copa*.[1] In this manner the poet moves from the people through to the hero or *libertador*, while still describing the unity of the collectivity through the shape of the individual. The idea of the people coming together is reinforced further by the use of *copa* in the sense of *copa de árbol*, i.e. head of a tree. This link with *árbol* brings in a major image of the *Canto general*. The poet therefore alludes to both cup and tree in the same word. The cup reference shows the people's cries gathered together into one unity, the tree reference shows Tupac Amaru as the head or crown of a much larger whole, i.e. *pueblo*. He is the crown of *árbol-pueblo*, but this is not intended in any hierarchical sense. The formation and organization of *pueblo* is compared to the formation and organization of a tree with all its parts, and the growth of *pueblo* is akin to the growth and spreading forth of a tree with its roots in the soil. This theme receives its most detailed treatment in the opening poem of *Los libertadores* (i. 378–80), where the poet shows the continual manifestation of *pueblo* and unity, opposed to its disappearance and disunity enforced by others, as a tree continually flowering and then being broken up by the enemies of *pueblo*. The movement of armed revolt in this poem is therefore described in terms of unification and the bringing together of scattered parts, as exemplified in the image of *copa*.

---

[1] The first poem in the *Canto general* describes man in terms of *copa*:
> El hombre tierra fue, ...
> copa imperial o sílice araucana.
>   (i. 319)

The shape of the ocean is also described in these terms:
> Tiempo, tal vez, o copa acumulada
> de todo movimiento, unidad pura ...
>   (i. 654)

When the land is dominated or taken over by a minority, the body of *patria* is broken and divided up. Therefore when *pueblo* come together to restore *patria* or reclaim their environment, the imagery reflects the coming together of scattered parts:

> . . . .
> se unieron los viejos cuchillos,
> y la caracola marina[1]
> llamó los vinculos dispersos. (i. 402)

The armed resistance and unity which has been built up or regrouped is now broken up because of the defeat of Tupac Amaru. The division of *pueblo* is paralleled by the collapse of a fortress wall into its component parts, and also by the quartering of the body of the leader, which symbolizes *pueblo* and *patria* as a whole.[2] Finally the image of a light or a dawn is rudely snuffed out. The final lines demonstrate how the unity and light of Tupac Amaru lives on as an example to future *libertadores*. The poem as a whole exhibits an astonishing coming-together of parts into wholes, and the reverse process of wholes back to parts. The body of Tupac Amaru is the body of *pueblo* and the body of the continent raped and divided by the Spanish *conquistador*. This image of breaking up, dividing, and dismembering is a continuing one in the *Canto general*, and it is always contrasted with the *unidad* and *forma* of *pueblo* and its own heroes.

From the beginning of *Los conquistadores* (i. 349–77) one side divides up, the other—restores a harmonious and natural *unidad*. The process of division and dismembering brings with it an atmosphere of silence and death.

> . . . .
> se apuñaleaban repartiéndose
> las traiciones adquiridas,

[1] There is another mention of *caracola* in i. 683. Here again reference is made to its use as a trumpet, an example of a part of nature being used by man for fruitful purpose:
> La caracola del tritón retuvo
> la distancia en la gruta del sonido . . .

The list of molluscs in i. 683–4 needs to be studied in great detail, for the poet incorporates many literary and social references in the list of sea-shells. Many of the references are only comprehensible to an expert on the subject. Neruda has collected vast numbers of these shells; see M. Aguirre, op. cit., pp. 164–7.

[2] This process is exactly similar to the part that the wall and the stones play in the collective references of *Alturas de Macchu-Picchu* (i. 335–48). The wall survives, leading the poet through to the survival of *pueblo*; see also i. 426:
> tú eres el muro hecho de nuestra sangre,

THE SOCIAL AND HISTORICAL PLANES

> se robaban la mujer y el oro,
> disputaban la dinastía.
> Se ahorcaban en los corrales,
> se desgranaban en la plaza,[1]
> se colgaban en los Cabildos.
> Caía el árbol del saqueo
> entre estocadas y gangrena.
> De aquel galope de Pizarros
> en los linares territorios
> nació un silencio estupefacto.
> Todo estaba lleno de muerte . . .
> (i. 365–6)

Here the negative images of rape, cupidity, treason, division, corruption, silence, and death are all paraded.[2] The continual movement between disintegration and integration is really the fundamental idea of all social references in the *Canto general*.

The passages examined above illustrate therefore the ordered and structured way that the poet represents social conflict and the importance of order, form, light, structure, and other related attributes when describing *pueblo* and *patria*. Because of this he almost always refers to *pueblo* in words such as *unidad, orden, forma, estatura*, and the central image around which all the other attendant images revolve is that of a body or unity being broken up by the enemy of *pueblo*. Among the very first descriptions of the Spanish *conquista* is the following, that of the fall of Cuba:

> Cuba, mi amor, te amarraron al potro,
> te cortaron la cara,
> te apartaron las piernas de oro pálido,
> te rompieron el sexo de granada,
> te atravesaron con cuchillos,
> te dividieron, te quemaron.
> (i. 350)

The image of division of a body is continued in terms of the robbing of life, and the rape of a woman. This last image is

[1] This line is missing in the 1968 *Obras completas*. It appears, however, in all previous editions.
[2] Images that refer to a division or breaking-up of a unified body occur continuously. See i. 350, 361, 363, 365, 369, 372, 379, 398, 401, 402, 425, 437, 464, 473, 475, 478, 498. In i. 648, *Patria te quieren repartir*, we have:
> Quieren quitarme patria bajo los pies, desean
> cortarte para ellos como baraja sucia
> y repartirte entre ellos como carne grasienta.

consistent with the equation of the form of the continent with the female form.[1] Moreover, it introduces another set of opposed images into the theme of social conflict. Those who seek to take away the land from *pueblo* and divide it up amongst themselves are compared to men who rape a woman, whilst *pueblo* and its heroes or *libertadores* are in a continual and intimate relationship with the earth, which is compared to normal and fruitful sexual relations. As we have already shown, every *libertador* is both a father and a son of *tierra*. This relationship between *pueblo* and *tierra* as a normal fruitful sexual intercourse, with the consent of the woman, contrasts as it were with the senseless, violent possession of the earth by the *conquistador*, the colonialist, the imperialist, and the oligarchy. The *libertador* and *pueblo*, be they Indians or Europeans, have an altogether different relation with *tierra*.[2] This relationship produces sons, and however much the others may try to possess or divide the land, they will never possess it in the harmonious and fertile way that is the privilege of *pueblo*. Such an interpretation suggests that the land is far from passive, and that nature allows itself to surrender only to the man whom it considers the true beneficiary of its fruits and delights.

Recently some writers have chosen to see in the land and the Spaniard the opposition of Indian and Spaniard or female and male respectively. This would make the land, the Indian, and the mother figure one set of indivisible associations, with the Spaniard and the father as another. Emir Rodríguez Monegal notes in his book on Neruda that the poet addresses America as a whole in terms of a woman or a mother, and he concludes from this: 'En todo el primer canto continúa este doble juego de identificación de América con la madre y del poeta con el fruto de esa tierra.[3] A su vez, lo español es identificado con el padre, extranjero y violador, el padre que entra arrasando y destruyendo, e implanta luego soberbiamente su semilla en el atropellado surco fecundo.'[4] According to this argument there is a subconscious dilemma in the mind of the poet about his origins of mixed Indian and Spanish blood, where he continually identifies the Indian with the land and

---

[1] 'America, for Pablo Neruda, is a perpetual battleground for the forces of men joined and committed in love to their land, and the forces of violent men seeking to rape and possess it' (Monguió, op. cit., p. 26).
[2] See i. 368–9, and the example of Recabarren discussed (i. 445–50).
[3] This refers to the first section, *La lámpara en la tierra* (i. 319–34).
[4] op. cit., p. 242.

THE SOCIAL AND HISTORICAL PLANES 117

the mother, passively enduring the violation of her body by the Spaniard. Unfortunately the picture is not so simple as that. The relationship between *Hombre* ⇌ *Tierra*, as previous chapters have demonstrated, is much wider in its implications. Rodríguez Monegal is correct when he equates *tierra* with the female, but *padre* is not just the Spaniard but also the Indian. The true father of the land is the man who can have a fruitful relationship with it, i.e. *pueblo* and *libertadores* made up of Indians and Spaniards alike. Rodríguez Monegal's argument would have Neruda deny his Spanish heritage, when the poet's view of history and *hombre* is far more comprehensive. *Pueblo* is not merely a racial collectivity; it is made up of Indians and Spaniards who, once they have settled in America, become just as much part of the continent as the Indians. Indeed, to be united or estranged in relation to the land is a cultural or social fact, not a racial one of Spanish versus Indian blood. In the *Canto general* the long line of *libertadores* who are all related to one another through a common attitude to *tierra*, *pueblo*, and *patria* include Indian, Negro, Spaniard, and Irishman.[1] Rodríguez Monegal's thesis is an attempt to interpret the themes of the *Canto general* in too narrow a fashion. The image of the *árbol del pueblo* which is so important to the themes of the poem shows the tree of the people as a concept which has its roots and springs forth from the soil. Since one *libertador*'s death occasions the birth of another in a continual human progression akin to the natural cycle, the role of *tierra* as the mother of all these people is far from passive. Nor can it be satisfactorily expressed as Rodríguez Monegal does: 'Neruda parece complacerse deliberadamente en negar todo lo español y reconocer solamente la raíz indígena del continente americano. Para él lo indígena es la matríz, la madre, la tierra en que hunde sus raíces el hombre de este nuevo

---

[1] See *Los libertadores*, i. 378–459. Especially Cuauhtémoc (1520), i. 380–1; Lautaro (1550), i. 389–93; B. O'Higgins (1810), i. 404–6; San Martín (1810), i. 407–9; Toussaint L'Ouverture, i. 423–4. These are all *libertadores* who personify the mixed racial origins of *pueblo*. The Indian–land–mother thesis has received its most famous treatment in Octavio Paz, *El laberinto de la soledad*, 4th edn (F.C.E., Mexico, 1964); see especially pp. 55–74. The subject is also discussed by A. P. Hogg in an unpublished thesis, 'The search for identity in post-revolutionary Mexican writing' (London, 1967), pp. 121, 237, 387 ff. The topic has become a fashionable one in Mexican thought, and has been used as an argument to assert the *Indianism* of America in relation to the Spanish or European heritage, which is considered alien and not authentic.

mundo.'¹ The crucial point is that *tierra* is not just *indígena* in the poem, since the tree representing *pueblo*, which grows out of the soil, displays a racial composition that is decidedly mixed. *Madre* is not necessarily Indian but a figure equated with land, which is a different matter altogether.² The description of the Spaniards as men who rape the earth is emphasized only because they are conquerors and enemies of *pueblo*, not because they are Spaniards. The contest between Spaniard and Indian is the forerunner of the struggle between *pueblo* and *oligarquía* described in the remaining sections of the *Canto general*. The simplification of history into a perpetual contest between good and evil is not so important as the relationship of order *v.* disorder or natural *v.* unnatural, and unity *v.* disunity, described so far. The image of the woman as the earth in intimate communion with *pueblo*, for whom she bears a long line of sons, is continually opposed to the woman seized by rapists who can never really possess her with consent because she belongs to another. This image presents a far more complex relationship and a richer pattern of references and associations in the *Canto general* than the conflict of Spanish *v.* Indian, on a racial basis.³

An illustration of this important fact is the description of the oligarchies that rule the countries of America after the Independence from Spain. These oligarchies give rise to a peculiarly characteristic set of images, which correspond to the fact that these are all people of America who have perverted that rightful inheritance. This allows the poet to present images of unhealthy graftings and perversions of the natural order of America. The main source of these images is to be found in *La arena traicionada* (i. 460–517), where the poet introduces the long list of dictators (many of Indian blood) with a correspondingly apt scene of disorder, perversion, and unnatural events:

<blockquote>Sauria, escamosa América enrollada</blockquote>

[1] op. cit., p. 241.

[2] The passage in i. 368–9 clearly shows the role of Indians as *padres* in relation to *patria*.

[3] The Spanish–Indian and male–female connection put forward by Monegal (op. cit., pp. 241–5) is clearly meant to show that Neruda's mixed racial origins are still apparent in his attitude to his mother and father, and especially to women in general. This mixture of the sexual, social, and psychological is undoubtedly due to the influence of Octavio Paz who sees in the modern Mexican an exaggerated *machismo* in front of the woman, in order to take over the role of the Spaniard and compensate for the passivity of the Mexican Indian in the face of the Spanish *conquista*. See *El laberinto*, pp. 55–74.

> al crecimiento vegetal, al mástil
> erigido en la ciénaga:
> amamantaste hijos terribles
> con venenosa leche de serpiente,
> tórridas cunas incubaron
> y cubrieron con barro amarillo
> una progenie encarnizada.
> El gato y la escorpiona fornicaron
> en la patria selvática.
>
> (i. 461)

Here, the structure of images shows clearly that the dictators arise out of the American soil like *pueblo*. However, the natural birth of *pueblo* and *libertadores* out of *tierra* is contrasted, in this case, with the emergence of life out of an unnatural sexual union in an environment of mud and slime. The image of the serpent links up with a similar reference in the first section of the *Canto general* (i. 323).[1] Here there is no reference to America in healthy natural terms. *Sauria* is a large lizard with a coarse scaly body, and this animal is compared to America, but only as a perversion of the *crecimiento vegetal*, i.e. the healthy natural growth of *pueblo* and *patria*. This scaly America gives birth to sons who are the complete opposite of *libertadores*, since they emerge out of the bogs and swamps and not the fertile earth. They are covered in mud and are a *progenie encarnizada*, i.e. both covered in blood and bloody by nature. The whole picture is summed up by the striking image of evil and unnatural sexual union in the last two lines, which contrasts with the union of *pueblo* and *tierra*. The notion developed by these images is that these people are akin to animals or plants that live off the growth of the healthy plants, like weeds or lianas, sucking and squeezing the life out of them. The possibilities for social reference in such images are obvious. When describing the Chilean upper classes, for example:

> . . . . .
> flores carnívoras, cultivos
> de las cavernas perfumadas,
> enredaderas chupadoras

---

[1] Y en el fondo del agua magna,
como el círculo de la tierra,
está la gigante anaconda
cubierta de barros rituales,
devoradora y religiosa.

> de sangre, estiércol y sudor,
> lianas estranguladoras,
> cadenas de boas feudales.
>
> (i. 477–8)

Here the images of unnatural and evil growths wrapped around the *crecimiento vegetal* of *pueblo* are continued, and the imagery implies that these people are intrinsically evil as well as unnatural. But the idea of the strangling of the life of *pueblo* receives its most effective treatment in the poem addressed to the Anaconda Copper Mining Co. (i. 490–2), where the poet describes the foreign company as an anaconda wrapped around the Chilean worker and squeezing the life out of him. Here, the imagery connects effectively on the natural, social, and historical planes. For it was in the opening descriptions of the landscape that the anaconda first made an appearance (i. 323), both as a serpent in the Garden of Eden, and as a reference to the arrival of the Spaniard and the Catholic religion.[1] Now, several centuries later, the image shows the role of the Spaniard and false religious forms assumed by the North American imperialist and his false economic forms. The imagery obviously indicates that, like the anaconda always to be found in the bottom of the water, these tyrants arise out of the soil of America with no outside help:

> De las antiguas cordilleras salieron los verdugos
> como huesos, como espinas americanas en el hirsuto lomo
> de una genealogía de catástrofes; establecidos fueron, ...
>
> . . . . . .
>
> Desde las cordilleras como bestias huesudas
> fueron procreados por nuestra arcilla negra.[2]   (i. 514)

Over all, the tyrants of America imply the imagery connected with *libertadores* and *pueblo* in reverse; in the descriptions of the

---

[1] The wider implications of the anaconda or serpent are not merely Catholic. Another possibility may be the false gods of the Aztec religion, especially the deity *Quetzalcoatl*, or the plumed serpent. For a comprehensive account of this deity, its origins and significance, see I. Nicholson, *Mexican and Central American Mythology* (London, 1967), pp. 78–94. The snake was a common motif in pre-Columbian architecture and costume in general (see Vaillant, op. cit., pp. 71, 167, 232, 236). In Westheim there is a suggestion that the serpent is the basis of all pre-Cortesian (i.e. Mexican) design. It may also be linked with the undulating shape of waves and mountains, an important area of association in the *Canto general*. See P. Westheim, *The Art of Ancient Mexico* (New York, 1965), pp. 102–6.

[2] Another treatment of this theme can be found later on in *Los gusanos del bosque* (i. 647). See also *Brasil* (i. 507).

dictators, the imperialists, and the oligarchies as a whole the poet moves from a natural order to an unnatural one, from unity to disunity, from life to death. There are further images of darkness which indicate a movement from the light of *pueblo* to the darkness and night of social disorder and injustice. The description of the Paraguayan dictator, El doctor Francia, for example:

> Solitaria grandeza en el salón
> lleno de espejos, espantajo
> negro sobre felpa roja
> y ratas asustadas en la noche.
> (i. 462)

The description emphasizes the lack of the people's presence in the person of the *verdugo*, as opposed to the presence of the collectivity described in the figure of a *libertador* like Recabarren (i. 445–50). The image of darkness is continually opposed to the light of *pueblo* in the darkness of the rats, the night which envelops the whole scene.[1] The dictators stifle the life of metals, shut doors, and darken the house:

> Pero los brujos matan los metales
> de la resurrección, cierran las puertas
> y entenebrecen la morada
> de las aves deslumbradoras.
> (i. 467)

The darkness of the description is to be equated with the death that prevents the light and life of *pueblo* from asserting themselves, and the colour of the bird-plumes from showing through: these symbolize the natural order shut out. This conflict of light stifled by darkness is developed at length in the social references of the *Canto general*, and similar examples can be deduced from other sets

---

[1] Another example of darkness to describe social disorder:
> ... la noche establecida
> como una cátedra, devora
> los capiteles miserables
> salpicados por el martirio.
> (i. 463)

See also i. 464, 466–7, 469, 474, 480, 493, 506, 507, 509, 510, 517. This last reference shows *pueblo* asserting itself over darkness:
> ... sube tus lanzas a la aurora,
> y en lo más alto deja que tu estrella iracunda
> fulgure, iluminando los caminos de América.

of opposites, such as silence *versus* speech, where the dictators stifle the speech of *pueblo*.¹ Referring to the dictatorship of Argentina under Rosas (1829–49) (i. 463–5), the poet describes the disappearance of a voice to sing the unity of *patria*:

> Dónde huyeron tus trigos espumosos?
> Tu apostura frutal, tu extensa boca,
> todo lo que se mueve por tus cuerdas
> para cantar, tu cuero trepidante
> de gran tambor, de estrella sin medida,
> enmudecieron bajo la implacable
> soledad de la cúpula encerrada.
>
> (i. 464)

Here the body of Argentina is devoid of natural growth and life. The sound of the nation's voice, compared to a woman, a guitar, and a drum, cannot be heard. The poet employs the usual apostrophe to address the body of the nation, which is, of course, the body of *pueblo*; and the apostrophe is continued in *tu boca, tus cuerdas, tu cuero*, all gathered together in the verb *enmudecieron*. The following verse develops images of darkness and death, which add to the correspondingly negative images of silence. This verse also develops the opposition of land and sea or water and earth, discussed in the previous chapter. Here, the death and silence engendered by the unjust repression of *pueblo* are carried over the Andes (*la cinta de nieve compartida*) to Chile, like waves over the earth. This figure is in line with the comparison of mountains and waves which is common in the *Canto general*. The waves of silence are heard in Chile and the water of the waves becomes the *llanto estepario* of the people of Argentina. Thus, water and earth, separate elements, are recollected into the final image, where *estepario* is obviously a reference to the extensive Argentine steppes or pampas. The poet refers to the vastness of Argentina in the first line of this verse, when he addresses the nation as *planeta* and *latitud*.² The mingling of land and sea expresses the social con-

---

[1] See i. 510, where light *v.* dark and speech *v.* silence are mingled:

> ... en su idioma,
> cierra la boca castellana,
> cubre la luz de las palabras
> que allí circularon como un
> río de estirpe cristalina. ...

[2] In the opening poem of the *Canto general* (i. 319) the poet uses the same comparison, *las pampas planetarias*.

THE SOCIAL AND HISTORICAL PLANES

fusion and turmoil engendered by the Rosas dictatorship. Finally this disorder is revoked, and life, fertility, growth, light, order, and voice are restored. What was previously broken up is gathered together again. This is reflected in the imagery of the last verse of this section:

> Pero el pueblo y el trigo se amasaron: entonces
> se alisó la cabeza terrenal, se peinaron
> las hebras enterradas de la luz, la agonía
> probó las puertas libres, destrozadas del viento,
> y de las polvaredas en el camino, una
> a una, dignidades sumergidas, escuelas,
> inteligencias, rostros en el polvo ascendieron
> hasta hacerse, unidades estrelladas,
> estatuas de la luz, puras praderas.
>
> (i. 465)

As is usual when he is describing the emergence of *patria*, the poet associates the forms of *pueblo* and the forms of the landscape in *unidad*. This is evident in the opening line of this verse, where *pueblo* and *trigo* come together, and the social and the natural achieve a transcendental fertility and form that emerge upwards from out of the soil, with attendant images of social work (*escuelas, inteligencias*) and light resurrected. Note also how the order that emerges was submerged, i.e. *dignidades sumergidas*. This is a reference to the confusion of land and sea referred to in the previous verse. Here the water has cleared away, and order is restored, to reveal what was previously submerged in the natural and social disorder. The *unidad* between people and land is completed in successive descriptions of positive and fruitful shapes: *unidades estrelladas, estatuas de la luz*, and finally *puras praderas*; so the extensive plains of Argentina are reunited with their rightful people in harmonious *puras praderas*. This movement has burst forth from *tierra* like the growth of *trigo*, and the poet therefore associates the re-establishment of *pueblo* as a renewal, or the arrival of spring after the hard winter.

This passage shows quite clearly how the poet employs related sets of opposites to express social themes in the *Canto general*: darkness *v.* light, silence *v.* sound, water *v.* earth, fertility *v.* infertility, unity *v.* disunity. The social themes of the *Canto general*, therefore, are described by use of opposed sets of images, with a systematic network of associations and links with the other levels of reference in the poem. The constant breaking up and restoration of *unidad* on the social level is worked out in terms of the Body ⇌ Continent relationship, and the intimate and productive relationship that *pueblo* as a collective body has with the female form of *tierra*. This relationship is opposed by negative images of rape and infertility, where the enemies of *pueblo* try unsuccessfully to possess and divide up the soil and its component parts, such as the minerals in the earth. This enables the poet to use the technical device of enumerating parts of nature to illustrate either unity or disunity. The whole of the landscape can be described and collected together in the figure of a *libertador* of *pueblo*, as the example of Recabarren (i. 445–50) illustrated. Conversely, the parts of nature can also be enumerated to demonstrate that the natural order and its *unidad* with the people have been dispersed, as the example of Tupac Amaru clearly showed (i. 401–2). The two movements are well brought out in the example just quoted about Rosas and the dictatorship of Argentina (i. 463–5). When *pueblo* renew their relationship with *tierra*, all the positive images associated with this act are displayed in formal schema, so that the event has almost a ritual significance,[1] where *pueblo* collectively re-establish their original link with *tierra*, returning into the earth to be reborn.

Collective resistance to dictators and oligarchies is only one side of *pueblo*; the other equally important aspect of their activity is work. Here the *Canto general* records their enduring achievements. In pre-Columbian America, as the previous chapter described, it was not the priests and the rulers that the poet's references focused on, but the collective work and effort of the common people that built the Aztec pyramids and the walls of Machu-Picchu (see i. 330–2; i. 340–1). Work not only is a means of constructing permanent shapes, it is also a means of regaining contact with *tierra* to achieve the unity of *patria*, when man and earth are come together for a common end. On the social level this has obvious Marxist references for Neruda. Work is the physical transforma-

[1] See L.S., op. cit., p. 32. Here a comparison is made between ritual and games. In the latter, equal teams with the same rules try to bring about a destruction of this balance, i.e. both sides try to win, but 'The reverse is true of ritual. There is an asymmetry which is postulated in advance between profane and sacred, faithful and officiating, dead and living, initiated and uninitiated, etc., and the "game" consists in making all participants pass to the winning side by means of events, the nature and ordering of which is genuinely structural.'

tion of the natural environment for the benefit of the collectivity, who can use the minerals of the earth for their salvation on earth and achieve a unity that is perfect, like the perfection of metals.[1] The relationship between men and metals, as it has been shown so far, has deeper overtones than mere social comment. But social activity like work and collective resistance to unjust social forms are expressed in this manner in the *Canto general*:

> Aquí el hombre era vida que juntaba
> la intacta luz, el mar sobreviviente,
> y atacaba y cantaba y combatía
> con la misma unidad de los metales,
>
> (i. 618)

This expresses an ideal or perfect state, as can be seen by the familiar image of man as life, joining light and sea together into a unity comparable with the unity of metals.[2] But the subjective nature and meaning of work and the objective social condition of *pueblo* can express a glaring contradiction when brought together. Between the deep significance of the act of work in a mine, for example, and the pitiful social and economic condition of the worker, there is a very rich theme. The act of work is a renewal of contact with the soil and its benefits, which does not bring about any renewal or benefit to the worker who touches its fruits. This contradiction is brought about through the foreign ownership of the mines, which are worked for the profit of the imperialists, so rendering the act of work totally invalid. This topic is well brought out in a poem entitled *El oro*, from *Las flores de Punitaqui* (i. 613).

> Tuvo el oro ese día de pureza.
> Antes de hundir de nuevo su estructura
> en la sucia salida que lo aguarda,
> recién llegado, recién desprendido
> de la solemne estatua de la tierra,   5
> fue depurado por el fuego, envuelto

[1] For a fuller examination of Marxist theory and poetry see Thomson, *Marxism and Poetry* (New York, 1946).
[2] The unity of metals is used to make a social point, but Neruda links the *unidad* of *pueblo* with other natural forms, through repetition of the same word, which acquires both social and natural references; see, for example:

> Tiempo, tal vez, o copa acumulada
> de todo movimiento, unidad pura . . .
>
> (i. 654)

> por el sudor y las manos del hombre.
> Allí se despidió el pueblo del oro.
> Y era terrestre su contacto, puro
> como la madre gris de la esmeralda.
> Igual era la mano sudorosa
> que recogió el lingote enmarañado,
> a la cepa de la tierra reducida
> por la infinita dimensión del tiempo,
> al color terrenal de las semillas,
> al suelo poderoso de los secretos,
> a la tierra que labra los racimos.
> Tierras del oro sin manchar, humanos
> materiales, metal inmaculado
> del pueblo, virginales minerías,
> que se tocan sin verse en la implacable
> encrucijada de sus dos caminos:
> el hombre seguirá mordiendo el polvo,
> seguirá siendo tierra pedregosa,
> y el oro subirá sobre su sangre
> hasta herir y reinar sobre el herido.
>
> (i. 613)

In this poem gold receives a complex treatment, and the poet has recourse to a number of his fundamental relationships, in what is, superficially, a piece of social criticism. The mine is owned by the oligarchy or foreigners, who exploit the Chilean worker and his labour, and then take the produce of his labour away for their own benefit and profit. But the imagery and its structure lead through to wider and related planes of reference on the natural and historical levels. Furthermore, the overt social plane is mapped out with great subtlety. The theme of a social good being perverted by economic exploiters is again worked out through a set of opposites, particularly purity *v.* impurity. The gold is described as pure when it is inside the shape of the earth, or when it is being melted down by the hand of the worker, from raw gold mingled with earth, to pure gold ingots. The gold becomes impure when it emerges out of the earth's form, to be employed against the worker who has brought it up and purified it. Therefore the metal takes up a contradictory position towards the worker, owing to social and economic causes. This is the conclusion or moral that the poet draws in the last four lines of the poem. The purity of the gold and its related attributes of potency, fertility, and structure can only be realized when the worker and the gold come together, as they do, for example, down in the mine, or when the worker separates the earth from the metal by melting it down, and creates the pure gold ingot. The relationship between worker and mineral is brief, but for that moment they draw beneficial purity from each other. Here the poet is able to fuse together the positive aspects of *oro* and *pueblo*, and draw some conclusions about the forces of nature in relation to *pueblo*, which contrast with the actual negative social framework of the situation that the poem describes. Once *oro* and *hombre* are separated, the gold becomes defiled and impure, and the worker lives a life of misery and hardship which defiles and soils the purpose of his labour. This is all conveyed in the contrast produced when the purity of his work and the purity of his product become defiled as the metal becomes capital or profit for a minority, to be used against *pueblo*. This is the conclusion displayed in the last four lines, where the potential of the fertile union between gold and people through work, described in terms of *tierra* and growth in the soil, is perverted in lines 23 and 24 to *polvo* and *tierra pedregosa*. Thus a social and economic commonplace, the foreign exploitation of natural resources, receives here a deep natural and moral treatment.

The images that are used to describe the act of work, and the gold that results from these labours, show that within the framework of social criticism the poet has worked out as another theme the origin of *hombre* in nature, and his return to these origins through work. Developing this in more detail, line 1 states that the gold was pure once, in the beginning, when the gold had just been removed from the shape of the earth. The shape of the earth is described as *estatua*, a favourite shape of the poet's, used here to refer to the continent as a female form.[1] This makes sense, because it enables the poet to describe the working of the earth by *pueblo*, for a mineral, as a pure and fertile sexual union between man and woman or *hombre* and *tierra*. The social implication is that this intercourse is frustrated and defiled, since the gold that is born of this union is swallowed up by a *sucia salida* (line 3). In other words, birth is the act of sinking or entering into a dirty hole,[2] which robs

---

[1] See i. 655, 661-3, 676-8, 690-2. In these passages the sea, the shape of man, and man-made forms are all linked through *estatua*.

[2] *Sucia salida* is connected to Neruda's use of the word *agujero*, which almost

the nascent metal of its pure life and nobility, and renders it base and filthy. Furthermore, it can no longer help the father who brought about its birth out of *tierra*, and the natural birth as a result of the union of *hombre* and *tierra* becomes debased and perverted in the references to *sucia salida*. The day of purity was before this act, inside the earth, when the raw gold was touched and transformed by the sweat and the hand of the Chilean worker. Owing to a social situation, the act of birth which the worker brings about is transformed into a living death, because the gold is separated from its creator. When the worker is in contact with the gold he has life, fertility, structure, and hope for a positive and fruitful social order; but when the gold is taken from his hands, it is used for other, negative, purposes, i.e. against him.[1]

The first three lines of the poem define this conflict or antagonistic situation on all levels, with the opposition of *pureza* (line 1) and *sucia salida* (line 3). The following lines (4–7) develop the positive theme of purity gained through work, which transforms both the worker and the gold. The worker through his labour actually creates the purity and cleanliness of the gold, giving it a moral meaning in relation to the purity and cleanliness of his work.[2] This social creation with moral overtones, where the image of fire refers to the melting down and purifying of the raw gold, also compares with the natural creation of minerals in the beginning of time.[3] The use of *fuego*, too, refers to the wider theme of man's power over nature. Through the use of tools man has learned to control fire, and it was the control of fire that enabled him to work metals to

always refers to death and social misery. There are added references to rape and violation of the body of the continent. Other mentions of *agujero* are i. 341, 506, 647, 663, 668, 708. The word is also used in this sense in his earlier poetry; see *Las furias y las penas*, i. 268, and *España en el corazón*, i. 275, 285, 289, 292, 295.

[1] The role of minerals as active agents that can help to construct and transform *hombre* is a common topic in the *Canto general*; see i. 496:

> Yo apartaré tu arcilla de la tierra
> hasta que te construyan los metales
> y salgas a brillar como una espada.

[2] See Thomson, op. cit., pp. 13 ff. Work transforms the objective world because of the subjective attitude and act of the worker. This is what Thomson calls the 'dialectics of poetry'.

[3] See i. 656:

> Cuando se trasmutaron las estrellas
> en tierra y en metal, cuando apagaron
> la energía y volcada fue la copa
> de auroras y carbones, . . .

construct a civilization. The effort of work takes *hombre* into an intimate union with gold, which renders both parties pure and fruitful. The significance of work is like a ritual of rebirth, for by re-entering the mines *hombre* returns to the womb, or into the earth represented by the female form as a woman and a mother. Both these facets are represented here: first, there is the time of purity when men and women come together to produce *oro*; and second, there is the longer span, back to the time when the first man himself was actually born out of woman/*tierra*. This *regressus ad uterum* reinforces the idea of going back to the beginnings of time,¹ of being reborn through the action of work, which becomes a ritual re-enactment of man's connections and origins in *tierra*. Against the time of the present event the poet sets the larger time of the origins of man and his past achievements, where he has continually lost and regained contact with *tierra*. This renewal of contact with *tierra* is fundamental to the poet's vision of the world, for it is the prerequisite for the existence of *patria* and *pueblo*. This social reference of the *Hombre* ⇌ *Tierra* equation carries with it all the images of construction and fertility, displayed in this particular passage in lines 13–17. The purely social level has a further historical dimension, however; this life of *pueblo* and *patria* relates back to the origins of social man in his work and construction, and the natural creation of his work. The poet, in *ese día de pureza* in line 1, is referring to both man and gold and their continual relationship from the beginning of time. Gold only becomes fertile and strong when it is touched by man, and for the poet it is an effective way to refer to the origins of man, the unity of *pueblo*, the nature of labour, and the social contradictions that the use or abuse of *oro* can imply. This poem illustrates perfectly the active shaping force that gold is capable of achieving for *pueblo*, but as an ideal it is unrealized in this particular case. None the less, it remains as an essential part of the images associated with life, order, harmony, fertility, light, language, and all the other positive images that have been discussed in this chapter. *Unidad* in a social sense can come about only when the metals are used for the benefit of *pueblo*.²

[1] Eliade, op. cit., p. 79.
[2] Aquí el hombre era vida que juntaba
la intacta luz, el mar sobreviviente,
y atacaba y cantaba y combatía
con la misma unidad de los metales.
(i. 618)

These transcendental relationships between *hombre* and *tierra*, achieved through work which purifies and ennobles the man who does it, are therefore perpetually enshrined in the concepts of *pueblo* and *patria*, which are brought into existence by such shaping forces as the *unidad de los metales*. This was the case, for example, in the description of *pueblo* through Recabarren (i. 445-50), where the natural and social meanings of metals are deliberately mingled together by the poet:

> Y este habitante transformado
> que se construyó en el combate,
> . . . . . .
> este metal inalterable,
> esta unidad de los dolores, . . . (i. 447)

This is precisely the same as in the relationship between man and gold discussed in the present commentary. The purity of this union between man and metal is broken (like a birth where the child is snatched from the mother) in line 8.

In the following lines (9-17) of the poem the poet returns to discuss in more detail the nature of the work of *pueblo* and the contact between man and gold. As a result of the mingling of man and gold in a positive set of associations, where fruitfulness and life are mutually exchanged between *pueblo* and *oro*, the poet is able to generalize in lines 18 to 22 about the purity of man and metal, where *pueblo* can become *metal*, and *metal* can become a living creative force which helps to forge the unity of *pueblo*. The fact of the poem's social context prevents this unity from being objectively realized, although it is a relationship which can never be really broken for very long, for the man of *pueblo* is continually renewing contact with the minerals in the earth through his work. The unnatural social condition, however, robs him of the fruit of his intercourse with the earth. Because of this, man continues in his pitiful economic state, where the fruits of his labours are turned against him.

From lines 9 to 17, therefore, the contact of *hombre* and *oro* is described. The gold is in a larval state inside the earth, which is also womb-like. The gold is surrounded and touched by earth which is pure (line 9), and compared to the figure of the mother (line 10). Gold being in the earth or the womb of the woman, the poet links these images of earth, mother, and purity, which envelop gold, to the hand of *hombre*, which has similar attributes. This is because the hand of man has sweated and laboured to bring out this raw gold still covered with earth, and now man purifies it by melting it down into pure gold ingots. However, what concerns the poet in equating man and gold is the fact that the two are united through *tierra*. When the worker touches the ravelled-up gold ingot he touches the very fruits of the earth in a natural sense; to this must be added the obvious social references about *unidad de los metales* and the historical associations about the past work of man and his origins which were discussed earlier on. The references that compress all the dimensions of time (lines 13–17), particularly in line 13, apply to man and gold equally. The age of gold compares with the age of man, both geologically and historically. The act of labour compresses all the past efforts of man into this instant, just as the past geological layers of time are compressed into the purity of the gold inside the earth. This gold, and this hope of *hombre* in fashioning the gold, are developed in a series of related images: *cepa* (line 13), *semillas* (line 15), *racimos* (line 17). Here there is an implication of birth, life, and fertility springing from the fertile soil out into the open. The gold within the earth is like the seed planted, which bears fruit through the fertilizing action of *hombre*, in this case work, which unites him with the soil in a fertile relationship. The past, present, and future are therefore all united into a synchronic moment through the ritual of work, when *hombre* touches *tierra*. The images refer to the potential growth of constructive values which envelop gold. When *pueblo* touch the gold it is a natural earthly contact (line 9), which begins to grow into the tree or *árbol del pueblo*. When *pueblo* touch gold, therefore, they touch their own potential which the metal can help to realize, and they relive their origins in the womb of nature, by participating in a ritual manner in the first or original birth. Hence the deep significance of work in all aspects in the *Canto general*. Through the ritual of work *pueblo* return to their own origins, and are continually reborn through their efforts of labour. The poem's social message is made all the more effective by the antagonism between the original first birth of man in *tierra*, which was pure, and the birth of man today, symbolized in the creative act of bringing the metal out of the earth into a fruitless and sterile existence which causes death to the Chilean worker.

All these values which are contained in the images of *oro* and *tierra* are totally subordinated in this particular case to the social implications of the passage. This is because the objective social context within which this ritual act of work is performed completely negates, debases, and soils the act by taking the product away from the worker. The poet has enumerated what potential the act of work can subjectively unleash in the pregnant earth, but the description of the power of *tierra* as a creative force is centred on the objective social implications of the use of this force by man. The earth/woman yields herself to *pueblo* as she always does, but the fruit of this union is born eventually into the hands of unnatural and negative forces against *pueblo*. This does not invalidate the powerful associations which the poet is able to plot with his images when describing any act of work in the *Canto general*.[1] Despite the adverse social conditions under which *hombre* labours, work brings him into contact with the only positive forces that can, together with his own effort, construct *pueblo* and *patria*.[2] Thus, it is through contact and union with *tierra* and its parts (*oro* in this example) that man will bring about his own salvation. This enables the poet to mingle *oro* and *hombre* as mirror images of one another. Hence the description of *oro* within the earth (lines 9–10) is followed by a description of man touching the gold that begins with the word *igual* (line 11). The gold transforms and purifies man, and man equally invests the gold with his purity because it is worked by him. This relationship is developed in lines 18–22, where the two subjects, man and gold, try to retain contact with one another, and spark off a set of crucial images when they connect. The purity of the intercourse is developed in *sin manchar* (line 18), *inmaculado* (line 19), and *virginales* (line 20). This purity or virginity is not a lack of consummation, however. The gold and *pueblo* have united in *humanos materiales*, and *metal inmaculado del pueblo* (lines 18–20). Because gold is touched and transformed by *pueblo*, and vice versa, images of purity, virginity, and cleanliness are used by the poet. Furthermore, the fruit of this union will not last very long in this particular case. Again the mine becomes the passage[3] to the womb of the woman entered by

---

[1] Other examples, i. 330–1, 347–8, 440, 563, 571, 661–3.
[2] Thomson, op. cit., pp. 13–16.
[3] . . . . .
      ven, Ramírez, con tus abrasadas
      manos que indagaron el útero
      de las cerradas minerías, . . .
                               (i. 611)

her rightful possessor, *pueblo* (line 20), where the climax of intercourse reaches a climax of purity exchanged between gold and man, achieved through work.

The last four lines (lines 23–6) contradict this potential, they negate the purity and fertility of the images displayed in lines 13–17. The deep ritual of work and the positive forces that it creates are completely destroyed by the objective social situation.[1] The equation between *hombre* and *tierra* becomes dust and stony ground, as opposed to the fruitful images of the soil in lines 13–17. The gold that rises out of the earth is used to attack the bleeding body of *pueblo* (lines 25–6). The passage demonstrates by this final movement the impurity, violence, and death that mark the end of *oro* and, by implication, of *hombre*; this is despite the purity, peace, and life of the gold when it comes into contact with *pueblo* through work. This shows how the abuse of metal is the abuse of *pueblo*, for once the poem has linked these together, in lines 18–22, the possession of *oro* implies the possession of *pueblo*. The final images of blood and wounds are consistent with an atmosphere of rape and violence that contrast with the cleanliness and purity of lines 18–20.

The network of comparisons that are built up in the imagery of this poem between gold and man come together to make not just a social point, but several other related points as well. This particular passage illustrates in addition the many levels of reference in one image of the *Canto general*: i.e. *oro*. Here the movement of the poetry shows how the poet is able to establish a network of associations which are not merely associative meanings in this particular context. The context of this poem shows that images such as *oro*, *tierra*, and *árbol* contain in their over-all meaning references to other poems, that is a system of contextual allusions which can be discerned in the *Canto general*. This much is obvious if one studies the recurring display of similar images in relation to *pueblo* and *patria*, for example, and the images used to address the numerous *libertadores*. It is this profound set of relationships which are disturbed and alluded to by the apparently superficial and trite social message of the poem. The

[1] In Thomson, op. cit., p. 16, 'The world is still objectively the same . . . but his subjective attitude to it has changed.' The objective situation is in conflict with the subjective relationship that the worker has with gold. Thus the dialectics of a social situation are perfectly illustrated in the themes and images of the poem. Only *pueblo* can transform reality.

social activity and work of man is of the greatest consequence in the integral meaning of the *Canto general*. The action of labour leads *hombre* through to his natural origins, which are continually discovered by the present man and his ancestors. In other words, the worker experiences a sensation of being united with past events and achievements buried in the soil or the past, which he brings up or resurrects to the surface. Thus the activity of *pueblo* is reinforced not only by analogy with the activity and order of nature, but also with the achievement of previous individuals of the collectivity who have returned to the earth. This is the profound natural and historical reference in any social work or action of *pueblo* when they regain and renew contact with the soil. Hence the levels of reference of *tierra* and *oro* in relation to *hombre* acquire increasing complexity and density because of the social reference which relates to the profoundest themes of the poetry in the *Canto general*. The significance of work is well brought out in another context, which reinforces the extract at present under scrutiny:

> Detrás de los libertadores estaba Juan
> trabajando, pescando y combatiendo,
> en su trabajo de carpintería o en su mina mojada.
> Sus manos han arado la tierra y han medido los caminos.
> Sus huesos están en todas partes.
> Pero vive. Regresó de la tierra. Ha nacido.
> Ha nacido de nuevo como una planta eterna.
>
> (i. 571)

The unknown worker is brought to the forefront and given a name which is symbolic of the common man.[1] He is the hero behind great traditional heroes like Recabarren or Tupac Amaru; and it is through his activity, be it fighting or working, that he achieves this ritual contact with other men, both present and past. Through work, and contact with the soil and its parts, the achievements of past men are resurrected out of the earth and are reborn and fulfilled in the present. The man's body becomes the parts of

---

[1] The name of Juan the worker is a continuing one to symbolize the equation of *Hombre–Tierra*, and to describe the truly ordinary man, behind the famous names. See i. 347, 364, 553–71. This section is entitled *La tierra se llama Juan*. The significance of this has been noted by D. Puccini, 'Lettura del *Canto general*', *Società*, No. 4 (Turin, Dec. 1950), pp. 585–619.

the earth, and his achievements through collective work bear fruit in the *planta eterna* or the *árbol del pueblo*, which is so frequent a reference in the *Canto general*.

The *árbol* image and its particular associations are of the highest importance in the poem as a whole. Here the poet clearly unites the natural, social, and historical references in an image which works out the themes of each plane of reference in elaborate detail. The social argument put forward in the *árbol* image is only one plane or level of the integral meaning. All these references are contained in *árbol*, which occurs continuously throughout the *Canto general*. The most detailed statement of *árbol–pueblo* occurs at the beginning of *Los libertadores* (i. 378–80).

The immense themes of the perpetuation of *pueblo* throughout history, and the continual organization and unity of the collectivity, are defined and described by the flowering of the tree with roots in the soil, and the parts of the tree which are enumerated with clear social references. Here again, these references to themes associated with *árbol* are picked up continually throughout the *Canto general*. In the opening lines of *La lámpara en la tierra* (i. 321) the different trees are named and described:

> . . . . . .
> eran volumen terrenal, sonido,
> eran territoriales existencias.

Their earthly shape and life refer to the shape and life of man soon to be described. Further on in this section the tree acquires yet another meaning, when the Maya civilization is castigated by the poet for its religious sacrifices:

> Mayas, habíais derribado
> el árbol del conocimiento.[1]
> (i. 331)

Here the tree of nature becomes the tree of knowledge and also the tree of *pueblo*, which the Maya priests use for their own benefit. The tree, then, can combine many levels of reference in one context, especially as it symbolizes a fundamental relationship in any description of the Araucanian Indians, who are closest to the poet's own personal experience. The highly developed and sophisticated

---

[1] To the social reference of the tree of *pueblo*, the Biblical reference to the tree of good and evil in the Garden of Eden should be added. The fall of man from a paradisal state is brought about for social reasons, however.

cultures fade away, but at the end of *La lámpara en la tierra* (i. 333-4) the only people who remain are the Indians who were closest to nature, closest to *árbol*, *piedra*, and *tierra*. These images remain, therefore, as essential parts of the description of *hombre* in any part of the *Canto general*.[1]

The clearest statement of *hombre–árbol* is at the beginning of *Los libertadores* (i. 378–80), and it is worth looking at in some detail, because it shows how an image can act as an organizing point which holds together a number of major themes in the poem; these are clearly defined by the shape of the tree and its component parts. The tree is defined by the poet in a structural and dynamic manner: the former refers to its shape and architectural composition, which serve to indicate the shape of *hombre*, *pueblo*, and *patria* respectively; the latter refers to its continual growth out of the soil. In other words, the natural cycle of continual rebirth is compared to the human or historical cycle. This comparison enables the poet to bring in the related themes of historical time which has passed away; the death of individuals who die in the defence of *pueblo*, in the shape of the tree and its roots in the earth; or past layers of accumulated time. The individuals fall back into the soil to nourish the roots which keep the tree as strong and healthy as ever. The *libertador* who dies for the sake of *pueblo* and *patria* does not die in vain, but adds his effort and suffering to the eventual victory of *pueblo*. When the tree is re-formed or re-emerges out of the earth, it can be viewed as the eternal fruit of the union between *hombre* and *tierra*.

These multiple references of *árbol* illustrate a common process in the *Canto general*: that the many themes of the poem are organized or held together round images such as *árbol* and *mineral* (as was demonstrated above in the case of *oro*). These images are mobilized or displayed in a formal manner by the poet, and related sets of connections are worked out to illustrate main points of the *Canto general*'s theses. The arrangement of the component parts of *árbol* in relation to an interconnected set of references has an order which is genuinely structural, and which alludes in the

---

[1] The tree continues to stand for the unity of *pueblo* and the social knowledge that it brings. In the Spanish conquest the invaders bring down the tree (i. 366), but order and unity are restored by the Araucanians (i. 368–9), who are described in terms of *árbol* and *bosque*. Prestes is described as an *árbol* in relation to *pueblo* who are *bosque* (i. 450–3).

use of precise images to past and future events throughout the poem.

The first verse (see text, i. 378-80) defines the essential movement of the whole poem, where *árbol* is compared to *pueblo*, and the life-giving sap which flows from the ground through the roots to the leaves on the branches is connected to the heroes or *libertadores* of *pueblo*, who come out of the earth to flower as leaves on the trees. The collectivity as a whole becomes therefore *follajes*, and the tree, like the continent as a whole, becomes a living shape which can be either the body of one individual, say a particular *libertador*, or the poet himself. The tree can be the continent as a whole as well, for the sap which runs through the tree is like the blood in arteries of the body or rivers of the continent (i. 325). At any rate, the poet here moves about within his familiar range of references, which are continuous throughout this passage and the whole of the *Canto general*. The second aspect introduced by the poet in this opening verse is the confrontation of the leaves agitated by the wind. This has a perfectly natural reference to the leaves or seeds that fall back into the ground to fertilize the tree yet again; but the noise of the rustling leaves becomes the noise or the voice of the collectivity, transmitting its language or story back to the earth so that it will be remembered. Each leaf is one man, and the foliage as a whole makes up the collective voice or story, which is carried back into the ground to flower again and be communicated to the poet in the present. This relationship of *hoja–hombre* and *follaje–pueblo* is confirmed and developed in the fifth verse, where the poet describes each individual leaf as the lips of a man:

> . . . . . .
> y sus labios eran las hojas
> del inmenso árbol repartido, . . .
>
> (i. 379)

The poet defines *pueblo* as the sum of parts moving from *hoja* to *follaje*, which has its origins right back in the earth. He gives a voice to this collectivity, and this is illustrated by the noise of the wind striking the tree and rustling the leaves. Here Neruda manages to suggest the deep connections there are in the *Canto general* between natural sounds and human cries caused by past or present social injustice. This is a perfect example of the poet moving from the natural to the social plane. The wind can be viewed as an image on the historical plane, where the continual action of time causes the leaves to drop away into the earth.[1] The autumnal reference of falling leaves foreshadows the rebirth in the spring, and so out of the very condition of death there begins the new process of life, for the death of one leaf is the potential rebirth of another, as the seed falls back into the soil. Here the poet alludes to the death of *libertadores* and *pueblo* as a whole, who die throughout history defending the tree. This is also the first image used to describe the tree undergoing attack by another element. In the fourth verse the tree will be swamped by water, and in the fifth it will be attacked by fire. These attacks and punishments that the tree endures are compared to the attacks and punishments that lead to the enduring survival in nature and history of *pueblo*, who undergo all these trials and deaths which are a condition of survival. The death of a leaf need not be a reference to a violent death; the poet is able to relate each individual death to a collective death which endures and survives in history. This fact is extremely important, since the individual death only acquires meaning if it is related to the larger death of the collectivity or *follaje*. This process can be seen most clearly in the final sections of *Alturas de Macchu-Picchu*, for example (see i. 340–8). With the seed entering the earth, from whence the tree originally came, the poet completes the enumeration of the cycle on a natural, social, and historical plane. The reference to *la semilla del pan* is probably an attempt to integrate the seed of the future birth with the tree of *pueblo*, in a genuinely social image of life and fertility. This is achieved by linking *pan* and *semilla*, where the former is a human product made out of the natural and potential life of *semilla*. On the other hand, the poet may be alluding to the *árbol pan* or 'breadfruit tree' in a botanical sense; it is to be found in the tropical areas of America, and has a fruit similar in taste to bread. Although this is a possibility, the main reference of *árbol pan* certainly lies in the linking of the natural and the social, where *pan* is the bread or food of life

---

[1] For a similar use of voices and wind blowing through the trees see i. 368–9. The use of wind as a force which remains once the life has passed away can also be seen in i. 333. Here the poet foreshadows the survival in time of the tree of *pueblo*:

> Todo es silencio de agua y viento.
> . . . .
> No hay nadie, sólo son los árboles.
>
> (i. 333–4)

for *pueblo*, the fruit and the seed of the tree that falls back into the soil to be reborn as the tree. The eternal unchanging structure of the tree and the dynamic movement of the cycle are well brought out by the final two lines of this verse:

> hasta que cae la semilla
> del pan otra vez a la tierra.
>
> (i. 378)

The second verse proceeds to describe in more detail some aspects of the cycle that were mapped out in the verse above. The *semilla* which enters the earth is now described in a neat link as the dead individuals of American history. The movement of the poem has accompanied the fall of the seed into the ground beneath the tree. The sufferings of the past individuals are depicted as buried and assimilated into the structure of the tree, which feeds through its roots on the sacrifice made by the individual members of *pueblo*. The death of each *libertador* can therefore be linked to the birth of another, so that the imagery establishes a line of descent or continuity from *pueblo* in the Inca empire right down to *pueblo* today. This truth is of crucial importance, a guiding principle in our understanding of the themes of the *Canto general*, as Neruda himself pointed out when he was writing the poem in the 1940s: 'Muy pronto me sentí complicado, porque las raíces de todos los chilenos se extendían debajo de la tierra y salían en otros territorios. O'Higgins tenía raíces en Miranda, Lautaro se emparentaba con Cuauhtémoc. La alfarería de Oaxaca tenía el mismo fulgor negro de las gredas de Chillán.'[1] Because of this truth revealed to the poet, the death of every *libertador* has become part of the seed–tree–leaf cycle, which enables him to link events that are separate both in time and space into a neat structural order. In this poem, however, the dead are unnamed, for the poet wishes to illustrate the anonymity of individuals who achieve identity through the collectivity of the tree. The historical cycle that is compared to the natural cycle enters the earth to re-establish contact with the past, and to become part of the collective death of *pueblo*. The image that takes the poet's personal search back into the past, along with the collective link backwards, is in the word *raíz*, which the next verse, the third, proceeds to develop. But in this second verse the accumulated suffering of the ages is paraded as the food which provides a life for the tree. The line of verbs is interesting, for in

[1] Quoted in Silva Castro, op. cit., p. 96.

several cases the bodies of men are shown to be beheaded or broken up. The poet refers here to the body of *pueblo* defiled and broken up, which achieves unity once more when it enters the tree. Many of the references can be traced to specific *libertadores*, who are to be treated individually in the following section. For example, the *empalados sobre una lanza* is a reference to Caupolicán (i. 386), but the poet wishes here to allude to the death as an anonymous event in relation to an over-all process.[1] Each death is therefore an act with profound natural repercussions when viewed in the macrocosm of history and the cycle of the tree. Part of the movement of this whole poem is from the particular individual death to the general and universal life of *pueblo* as an enduring body. The death by quartering which follows further down in this verse refers to Tupac Amaru (i. 401–2); but in every case the death of an anonymous individual is viewed as a death that contributes to the life of the tree for the future. *Tierra* becomes the living repository of the past which nourishes the roots of the tree. As a result, any reference to *raíz*, *tierra*, or *semilla* must contain these historical themes. It illustrates, too, important earlier points that were made in connection with men who worked in mines in the earth. The poet connects the process of digging into the earth by *pueblo* with the same downward process of the tree spreading roots underground. In both cases the relationship of *pueblo* and *tierra* is described as beneficial, and in both cases the entry into the earth re-establishes contact with the past, renewing links that are constant throughout the poem. This is the *Hombre⇌Tierra* relationship, represented as a union on many levels, of which the tree is the fruit. The sequence of the tree-cycle described in the first verse—*tierra*, *semilla*, *raíz*, *tronco*, *rama*, *hoja*, *flor*—is one containing elements that can be referred to singly and still imply the whole cycle. Hence the significance of the following lines, which were studied earlier, when the poet describes a miner in the earth touching gold:

. . . . .
a la cepa de la tierra reducida
por la infinita dimensión del tiempo,
al color terrenal de las semillas,

[1] i. 386–9. The life and leadership of Caupolicán are worked out entirely in terms of the *árbol* image, and his death is the perfect illustration of the seed returning to the earth.

       al suelo poderoso de los secretos,
       a la tierra que labra los racimos.
                         (i. 613)

Here, the imagery links the act of work in its social and historical context with the network of images associated with the tree-cycle, and therefore reinforces the poem's meaning.

In the third verse the movement up from roots to tree is developed by the poet when he shows the suffering of the people in a universal dimension. The standard *tierra, semilla, raíz, tronco, rama, hoja, flor* cycle is developed by analogy with *salitre, sangre, lágrima*, where in each case the roots of the tree obtain some fruit or benefit from what might appear to be a sterile or negative event. This reinforces the role of the tree as an agent that assimilates and transforms disorder and individual death into a collective unity which helps to maintain the *árbol–pueblo*. *Martirio* leads to *salitre*, and *sangre/lágrimas*[1] leads through the roots and up the tree to *flores*. Here a new set of relationships confronts the reader in relation to *árbol*; these are the organizational, transformational, and ordering energies of the tree or collectivity used in turning suffering, which is negative and sterile, into flowers which are beautiful and fertile, since they have *fruto* and *semilla*. This links up with other examples which speak of *la flor organizada del pueblo* or *Las flores de Punitaqui*.[2] The active energies of the

---

[1] Water and blood are contrasted and united in the structure of the tree, linking the blood, i.e. arteries, of the body, and the rivers of the Continent, in the structure of the tree. In i. 325 the Continent's shape is addressed with all these references:
           Amada de los ríos, combatida
           por agua azul y gotas transparentes,
           como un árbol de venas es tu espectro...

[2] i. 383:
           Fue la razón tu material titánico.
           Fue flor organizada tu estructura.
and i. 612:
           Flores, flores de altura,
           flores de mina y piedra, flores
           de Punitaqui, hijas
           del amargo subsuelo: ...

See also the same set of references from root to flower in *La ola* (i. 670). The movement of energy that comes up from the bottom of the sea and explodes in a wave is like the movement from the roots through the tree to the ordered display of beauty, light, and harmony in a flower. The movement of the wave is linked through the flower to the social and historical themes in the *Canto general*.

collectivity are contained in the permanence and beauty of the flower, which is the end product of the cycle, before it becomes fruit or seed which falls back into the ground. The fruit can be enjoyed by man, and the seed contains the essence of future birth and growth out of the earth. The movement of life from the roots through the tree has been developed in a further reference to the *arquitectura* of the tree. Here the structure of the tree and its ordered activity are compared to the shape of a human construction, such as the city of Machu-Picchu for example. In *Alturas de Macchu-Picchu* (i. 341) there is a similar movement from architecture to tree, when the city is described as *la exactitud enarbolada*. In this case the permanence of the city's architecture leads the poet through to man and the permanence of his collective effort, which can be discerned in the shape of the city. Earlier in the same section (i. 341) the wall of the city made up of stone blocks comes together like a rose and its petals. Thus, when the poet refers to the tree and the cycle that moves from seed to flower, the reference is either to the structural qualities of flower or tree, i.e. to parts that come together to form a unity, or it is to the dynamic perpetuating qualities of the tree's cyclical rebirth out of the soil. Thus tree and flower have both permanence and organization. The poem shows this permanence of the *árbol–flor* in a little more detail by describing them as plants which sometimes bloom on the tree and sometimes are buried in the soil; but their petals periodically reappear, to cast a light as universal as that of the planets. The flower which blooms on the tree is not meant to represent an individual, and is not inconsistent with the use of *hoja*. The flower should be viewed as the end product or achievement of the tree in terms of beauty, permanence, and organization: this is the flower of *pueblo*, which is achieved through its own efforts and sufferings. The tree transforms *salitre*, *sangre*, and *lágrimas* into *flores*, giving a life and a permanent monument to the transient sufferings and death of each individual described in the second verse. The *flor* of the third verse is the climax of the process described in the second verse. The cycle continues to be developed, therefore, with *hoja* and *flor* occupying quite distinct positions in the tree's frame of reference.

The fourth verse develops the cycle even further, for here man is described plucking the fruit off the tree and passing it from one man to another. Here the legacy of the past is picked up by the present man in the shape of a fruit or flower, and planted once again by him. The fruit here is shown leading the present man back to the earth, and teaching him the buried lessons and achievements of the past. Hence the present man acts in the light and knowledge of past events, which are all enshrined in the structure of the cycle and the fruit of the tree. The events and achievements of the past, consistent with the image of the tree's cycle, bear fruit in the actions of the present. The magnitude of the plant's growth is dramatically enlarged by the reference to the stars:

. . . . . .
y de pronto, abrieron la tierra,
crecieron hasta las estrellas.
(i. 379)

This links up with the planet–flower reference in the previous verse, and as a result the poet enlarges the tree's cycle to universal proportions. But the poet is able to refer to his themes in the widest possible sense without destroying the impact of his initial image built around the shape of the tree. The flowers on the tree shine like the planets and stars, and the actions of *pueblo* are again bathed in images of light, while the size and shape of the tree and, of course, *pueblo* stand defined from the roots in the earth to the stars in the heavens.

There is a clear distinction to be made again between the flower on the tree and the fruit. The fruit is, of course, the last stage before returning to the earth to become *semilla*. The fruit is the achievement of the past man, picked up by the present, and replanted in the earth. There is therefore a continual union between the past and the present, when the present man plucks the fruit from the tree. *Flor*, by contrast, is the suffering of each individual, which flowers into the collective order and beauty. The wall at Machu-Picchu is *la rosa permanente* (i. 341), for example, but it must return to the earth as fruit or seed to flower again today. Hence the poet moves from the wall, which is a flower, to the seed, which is man. Hence also the rich historical references that the poet works out in the succession of *libertadores* who are continually taking the fruit and returning on their death to the earth, to fertilize the tree with their blood.[1] Such a succession of images

[1] See *Los libertadores* (i. 378–459), where this relationship is worked out in some detail: i. 386–9 (*Caupolicán*), 389–93 (*Lautaro*), 393–4 (*Valdivia*), 401 (*Comuneros del socorro*), 401–2 (*Tupac Amaru*), 402–4 (*América insurrecta*),

has obvious connections with the relationship of *Hombre* ⇌ *Tierra* in male–female terms described elsewhere, for the fruit of the union between man and earth is the tree, whose fruit in turn is picked up by *pueblo* and transferred back to earth. It is *pueblo* who are continually fertilizing the earth; this is consistent with the choice of the images *magnolia* and *granada*,[1] which refer to the fruit of the tree rather than the flower. Both these fruits are used by the poet for other convincing details that support his arguments: they are both globular in structure and of some considerable size. The flowers of the *magnolia* tree are not only globe-like in configuration, but also of a vivid white colour, so the poet is able first to invoke the planet image, through the colour and shape of the *magnolia* flower, whose whiteness shines with a light that has associations of goodness and life; and second to develop the rebirth of a whole world or planet from the tree-cycle, through the shape and content of the *magnolia* and the *granada* fruit as a logical continuation of the flower.

The movement of the images, which has made both the structure and the cycle of the tree progressively broader-based and more universal in reference, continues to be developed in the fifth verse. Here the tree is described fairly obviously in terms of freedom, but more interestingly in the high–low relationship of *tierra-nube*, which foreshadows the earth–water equation further on. By an index of scale the tree is now clearly established in size, ranging from the earth to the heavens. In the fifth verse the poet brings together the earth and the air (*tierra-nube*), the fire and the water, all mingled together in the image of the tree. The tree becomes linked with differing elements of the cosmos, which point to the traditional four elements of earth, air, fire, and water.[2] The poet combines these with images of aggression and survival, and with

---

407–9 (*San Martín*), 428–9 (*Martí*), 450–3 (*Prestes*), and finally 457–9 (*Llegará el día*). On all these occasions reference is made to the tree cycle.

[1] i. 350; *Cuba* is described as a raped female:

> . . . . . .
> te rompieron el sexo de granada, . . .

See also i. 394, where the death of Valdivia is described in terms of *granada* and the tree-cycle as a whole.

[2] C. Meléndez, op. cit., p. 22, mentions the importance of the four traditional elements in Neruda's poetry. This is before the *Canto general*, however. Meléndez is right in saying that earth and water are far more important than fire and air.

THE SOCIAL AND HISTORICAL PLANES 145

instruments made by man, so that the imagery achieves a harmonious synthesis of the natural and social planes of the poem:

> El árbol tierra, el árbol nube,
> el árbol pan, el árbol flecha,
> el árbol puño, el árbol fuego.
>
> (i. 379)

Here *pan, flecha, puño* are human instruments or qualities for survival and life. The poet picks up the earlier reference to *pan*, which aptly combines the natural bread-tree with the tree that symbolically gives bread to man. This idea of many kinds of trees in a natural sense neatly reflects the universality of the tree, i.e. earth-tree, cloud-tree, bread-tree, arrow-tree, etc. The catalogue of trees might be a natural catalogue, and here the poet effectively brings the natural and logical references of the tree into one set of images. The reference to *pan* completes the possible list of fruits that the tree bears—*magnolia, granada, pan*; but the latter has far wider references as the 'bread of life' in general, produced by the collectivity in its continuing communion with the earth.[1] The *puño–fuego* opposition refers both to the human strength of man and to his use of fire as a natural resource to overcome and transform nature for his own benefit. Finally, the high–low opposition in *tierra–nube* is contained in *pan–flecha*, where the bread springs from the tree and the arrow soars upwards into the sky, and indicates a weapon of resistance used by *pueblo*. The burning and hot qualities of *fuego* are immediately contrasted with the tree assailed by the opposing forces which sweep over the land like a flood. Here the poet again parades a consistent set of opposed images: the tree and its attendant images of life, light, and fertility are drowned by the water, darkness, and death. Once again we are presented with the basic land–sea equation, which is so important in the *Canto general*.[2] Here the poet is able to continue his catalogue

---

[1] i. 620 combines the creative force of nature and social man:

> Sobre esta claridad irá naciendo
> la granja, la ciudad, la minería,
> y sobre esta unidad como la tierra
> firme y germinadora se ha dispuesto
> la creadora permanencia, el germen
> de la nueva ciudad para las vidas.
> ... patria
> amasada por manos metalúrgicas, ...

[2] Machu-Picchu was shown to survive the forces of destruction like a reef which kept above the water and the waves (i. 339, 341, 344). This association

of elements (earth, air, fire, water) around the tree, and also to illustrate human struggle in the conventional confusion of elements. Here the poet also shows the enduring structure and cycle of the tree which survives the temporary flooding; the water refers both to the action of time, which can bury and blot out the memory of the past, and to *pueblo* in the minds of people today.[1] But the reference also contains clear social argument about the contemporary political situation, where the tree of *pueblo* is drowned by the negative forces of imperialism, or the oligarchy. The tree and its survival are compared to the mast of a ship in a storm at sea being tossed about by the waters, but which juts out above the waves. The situation of confusion and doubt, when the skies are dark and the seas are swollen, with the ship at the mercy of the wild elements, is saved and restored by the mast or tree of *pueblo*. This image is effective to describe the *árbol–pueblo*, assailed by social torment and injustice: in terms of the natural order, thrown into violent and stormy confusion.

The sixth verse develops the structural properties of *árbol–pueblo*, where the tree is broken up and scattered by the anger and opposition of the enemies of *pueblo*. The fire of the previous verse, used for a beneficial purpose, now becomes the fire used against the tree, to try and burn it down. The list of elements enumerated that attack or affect the tree are air (*el viento estrella los follajes*), water (*lo ahoga el agua tormentosa*), and fire (*una ceniza amenazante*). The breaking-up and burning of the tree is followed by a coming-together of its broken parts. This process is described by the poet as a perpetual conflict, which the tree always survives, because the very action of attack on the tree generates new life from the roots in the earth that can never be removed. The ordeal of fire is yet another test that *pueblo* endure, and refers back to the second verse, where the list of people whose deaths contributed to the tree's growth included those burnt at the stake in the name of the

is a common one in the *Canto general*, where the waves are continually attempting to cover the land, and the poet draws support for his argument about the survival of man from the rocks on the coast, the city of Machu-Picchu, or the statues on Easter Island (i. 661–3).

[1] i. 319:
>Nadie pudo
>recordarlas después: el viento
>las olvidó, el idioma del agua
>fue enterrado, las claves se perdieron
>o se inundaron de silencio o sangre.

Catholic faith. The tree becomes the stake, but it endures and survives to be resurrected by the hand of *pueblo*. The breaking-up of the tree, leading back to its reconstruction, is neatly worked out, for the *ramas rotas* become the *brazos innumerables* which gather the fragments that are hidden away. Though the tree disappears and is broken up, it never dies, as the cycle always continues, so that it reunites into the *unidad* of *pueblo*, and flowers once again. The people are the fragments of the tree, and by coming together they rebuild the tree and renew contact with the earth through *raíces*. The collectivity acquires a voice through the *hombre–hoja* relationship, where the comparison is refined to *hojas–labios*. The tree becomes defined as the collectivity itself as well as the area that it inhabits, i.e. *patria*. All the surging wealth of natural phenomena and the themes that the landscape suggests are formally ordered and structured into the unified shape of the tree and its parts.

The final two verses address themselves in appeal to each individual that forms a part of *árbol* to defend and preserve its existence. In these verses the poet moves confidently about the tree, mingling natural, social, and historical references in depicting the relationship that brings together each man and the tree. The movement of these lines is governed by the imperative verbs, of natural life and activity, that urge the individual and the *árbol* to come together like man and woman. This relates to the larger relationship of *Hombre* ⇌ *Tierra* now described through the tree. *Árbol* is compared to the female-form/continent relationship in the *cabellera* image, which is both the foliage or crown of the tree and the hair of the woman.[1] The cycle of the tree is referred to, but in the intimate terms of a relationship:

> . . . . . .
> hunde la mano en las usinas
> donde su fruto palpitante
> propaga su luz cada día.
> (i. 379)

The individual enters into an intimate union with *tierra* and its fruit, through the active agency of the tree which produces the

---

[1] i. 325:
. . . .
como un árbol de venas es tu espectro
de diosa oscura que muerde manzanas: . . .

fruit that lights the world. The cycle results in the creation of fruit every day: and the image of light links up with a similar image in the third verse:

>   . . . iluminaron
>   sus pétalos, como planetas.
>
>   (i. 378)

The word *usina*[1] is used in the sense of a central generating machine that throbs with life and activity. Here the very life of the tree and the individual are united, as the final verbs in the next verse imply: *comparte las noches hostiles* and *respira la altura estrellada*. Doubtless the image also refers to the proper use of mechanical resources, which will bear fruit for man's benefit. The circle is now completed in its last details, as the poet enumerates the ordered union of the individual within the framework of the tree. The fruit of the *árbol–pueblo* is described, in a final image of light, by the word *esplendor*, and the individual now eats the bread and apple of the tree, which give him energy and life to defend the tree, from *copa* to *raíz*, against any attack. The frontier of *patria* becomes the very tip of the leaves, which is the limit of the poem's frame of reference. The final verse continues this catalogue of verbs that invite the individual to defend and share the benefits of the tree. The size of the tree takes on a universal scale in the final lines, as it reaches to the stars and grows from the centre of the earth. The poet has therefore obtained the widest and most universal reference through the tree. Finally, it would seem that man within *patria*, or within the limits of the tree, is now incorporated into the cycle of the tree; the poet urges him to guard the tree night and day:

>   .   .   .   .   .   .
>   comparte las noches hostiles,
>   vigila el ciclo de la aurora, . . .
>
>   (i. 380).

The difficult hostile nights are followed by the dawn of human hopes, but the individual must never relax his guard, for the tree is always menaced by natural and social forces, and thus the cycle goes on continually.

[1] See F. J. Santamaría, *Diccionario general de americanismos* (3 vols., Mexico, 1942), vol. iii, p. 244: 'En Argentina, conjunto de máquinas, establecimiento industrial, planta de elaboración y producción de algún artículo, o generadora de energía, o cosa similar.'

THE SOCIAL AND HISTORICAL PLANES 149

This poem has illustrated in some considerable detail the complex formal mingling of *tierra, aire, fuego,* and *agua,* displayed in a shifting set of relationships around the tree, where the poet by careful stages varies the size of the tree from that of a plant within a landscape to that of the universe as a whole.[1] By using the four elements the poet defines the scope of the poem's frame of reference, but always in relation to the tree, which is continually linked to *hombre,* so that the poet is able to illustrate several major themes at the same time on interconnected planes. That the achievements of *pueblo* should be viewed in terms of *árbol* reinforces the major theme of the *Canto general,* that man is made up of the parts of nature, which are in a continual state of separation from and relation with him, owing to social and historical forces as well as natural conflict. Here the poet shows, through one central image, how all these various levels are interconnected, and how it is impossible to view movement and disturbance on the social and political plane without referring to related planes. The poet achieves all these references through the structure of the tree, which is taken to pieces and compared to the collectivity, and re-formed at the end of the poem, its structure and cycle incorporated into the structure and cycle of *pueblo.* A list of the over-all relationships in this passage which illustrate major themes in the *Canto general* would include:

1. *The tree broken up and re-formed*: here the poet is able to describe the individual, *hoja,* coming together with other individuals to form a unity which is the tree re-formed. The tree becomes the logical equivalent of *pueblo* through *unidad, forma, estructura.* All these important words are used by the poet to describe natural objects and social groups, linked in this case through the image of the tree. The poet is able, therefore, to operate on the natural and the cultural plane, where the cultural is made up of natural elements used by man.

2. *The tree fertilized by the dead heroes of 'pueblo'*: the tree acts as a shape which gathers all the individual sufferings and deaths into one outline, i.e. the tree and its crown or *copa.* Because of this the poet is able to make a double set of references: (*a*) to a cup

---

[1] The Renaissance poetic tradition has numerous examples of the tree beset by natural forces. This figure was used for moral or amatory purposes, and Neruda can be set against this poetic tradition. See E. George Erdman Jr., 'Arboreal figures in the Golden Age sonnet', *P.M.L.A.* 84 (1969), pp. 587–95.

which gathers the tears and the blood in one unity, and (*b*) to the tree which drinks through its roots the tears and the blood shed by *pueblo* into the soil, to turn them into flowers and fruits which form the *copa* or head of the tree.[1]

3. *The tree as a fruit of the union between 'Hombre' and 'Tierra'*: here the poet gives a new meaning to the continuing relationship with the earth. As work or labour by *hombre* produces a whole set of life imagery, with attendant images of fertility and order, so the fruit of the tree is the product of an ordered structure that is natural and harmonious, which is compared in turn to *pueblo*. The tree is *pueblo*, and when *pueblo* and *tierra* are in intimate intercourse the fruit of the tree springs from the seed in the earth, just as gold in the earth is like a seed which will flower when it is touched by man through the act of work (i. 612–13).

4. *The tree as an enduring plant or unity which has to be continually defended*: here the poet is able to work out a series of interconnected relationships. The tree is one individual with limbs and a trunk; when that individual joins with other individuals to form *pueblo*, this also can be viewed as a tree, i.e. each individual becomes a leaf on the tree. The third possibility is the relationship *árbol–patria*, where the tree becomes the sum of land and inhabitants within that territory, which has to be preserved and defended if it is to survive. Finally, the tree becomes the shape of the whole world and all natural forces. This movement can be described as a progression from the individual to the collectivity, on ever-increasing planes of generality, through the medium of the tree, which can be compared to the continent of America as a whole; thus we get a progression:

hombre——pueblo——patria——tierra——planeta

All the elements that are traditionally associated with the creation of the world are divided and ordered by the tree, so in a sense the tree may be regarded, in the detail of its structure and components, as a metaphor for the earth inhabited by man.

[1] *Copa* connects the shape of man and tree in the *copa de árbol* reference, and also in the cup reference which the poet continually uses to define man:

El hombre tierra fue, . . .
copa imperial o sílice araucana.
(i. 319)

Como la copa de arcilla era
la raza mineral, . . .
(i. 330)

5. *The tree is continually reborn and gives forth fruit and flower*: here the poet establishes very clearly the crucial cycle of *tierra, semilla, raíz, tronco, rama, hoja, flor, fruto*, which enables the tree to be viewed as a dynamic force as well as a structural entity. This has most important consequences in the historical references throughout the *Canto general*. The onward march of historical events is only significant to the poet's universe, or equipment of imagery, in that these events are viewed with reference to a structural set of relationships and values which survive from the creation of America to the present day. From a critical point of view, the relationships illustrated by the tree are the important connections that Neruda tries to stress as recurring throughout history. The mere chronology, or order of events as a diachronic progression, is less important than the abiding link between *hombre* and *tierra*, and the way that history illustrates the continual manifestation of the unity of *pueblo* and its continual victory over opposed forces. The tree as a natural object survives, the tree when used as a conceptual tool to designate *pueblo* and *patria* also survives. Through the roots in the soil the poet is able to show that death and disappearance from life only serve to feed the present or future life, because these many little deaths reappear as the fruit and flower of the tree.

But what keeps the *Canto general* from losing any spatio-temporal qualities is the use of the same images, with the same relationships and references, at different moments in time, where the poet can allude to past or future events, and make any historical event give a true feeling of catching the whole sweep of time in one moment. It is important to note how this process or cycle, culminating in the flower and the fruit with roots in the soil, is used first to designate the efforts of men who build a shape, made of natural substances, which survives into the present; and second (in the process of the flower) to represent the visible part of a movement of life or energy which is continually reflowering. The first condition is fulfilled by the wall at Machu-Picchu and by the city as a whole, and the second can be usefully illustrated by the wave, which continually bursts from the depths of the ocean like a flower (i. 670).[1] The diachronic aspect of time is brought

---

[1] The city wall is referred to as a rose (i. 341), and the wave is referred to as a flower (i. 670). The two are brought together when the poet speaks of the city as 'Ola de plata, dirección del tiempo' (i. 344).

together in the synchronic structure of the imagery. The poet continually uses aspects of the natural landscape to reinforce social and historical arguments, which are contained in the recurring images of the *Canto general*, disposed into a series of relationships which, viewed as a whole, constitute a recurring structure that illustrates the major themes of the poem. This over-all structure, both synchronic and diachronic, which the image of the tree has defined, enables the form and the content of the *Canto general* to be defined as a whole through the organization of the imagery. This brings us to the final question of this chapter, namely the importance of the movement of history and historical change throughout the poem.

Neruda continually alludes to a discovery of his own identity in history, a personal discovery which must be set against the collective discovery of an identity throughout history for the *pueblo* of America as a whole. This double role of the poet as an individual and as a member of a group has already been mentioned in previous chapters, but it should be discussed in a purely historical context. The imagery, with its interconnected levels of reference, helps to communicate this fact to the reader. This process has been carefully plotted in the *árbol* image, where the tree with roots in the past is both the poet as an individual and *pueblo* throughout history. By successive planes of increasing generalization the poet incorporates himself into the collectivity, to become one of the leaves of the tree as a whole.

The theme of discovering an identity in history both as a person and as a member of a race has become a major preoccupation in Latin American philosophy, literature, and ideology in general. The study of history and the historical past has become for Latin American writers a means of philosophical analysis with which to interpret their present circumstances, and also a means to understand their true nature and capabilities for the future. Each writer has tried to describe what is distinctive about himself, and also to map out the distinctive characteristics of his country and its historical past. This is the case with Octavio Paz, who, in his *El laberinto de la soledad*, admits these problems to be more private than public. By examining the history and character of the Mexican, Paz is undeniably examining himself: 'Voy a insinuar una respuesta que quizá no sea del todo satisfactoria. Con ella no pretendo sino aclararme a mí mismo el sentido de algunas experiencias y admito que tal vez no tenga más valor que el de constituir una respuesta personal a una pregunta personal.'[1] So it is through the analysis of Mexican history, past and present, that writers and poets such as Octavio Paz have found a device for discussing personal and general experiences in one framework; in addition, they have managed to ask and answer questions that concern them as private individuals, and that are relevant to the continent of America as a whole. Put slightly differently, these writers have found a general framework within which to fit their own individual experiences, and they have been able to explain themselves in relation to some over-all frame of reference, where individual activity has a direct relationship to a constant set of general principles. Leopoldo Zea, the Mexican philosopher, has defined this process as an attempt to '... captar la llamada esencia de lo americano, tanto en su expresión histórica y cultural, como en su expresión ontológica'.[2]

This is well illustrated in the *Canto general* when, for example, Neruda asks:

> De dónde soy, me pregunto a veces, de dónde diablos
> vengo, qué día es hoy, qué pasa,
> ronco, en medio del sueño, del árbol, de la noche,
> y una ola se levanta como un párpado, un día
> nace de ella, un relámpago con hocico de tigre.
>
> (i. 373)

Here the poet's questions about his origins in time are immediately thrown open to the movement and shapes of nature in the familiar Nerudian manner. But in asking these questions, and in searching for a past that relates with his present circumstances, the poet also inquires on behalf of *pueblo*, whose past achievements acquire unity and language through the mouth of the poet. Neruda ritualistically becomes, in the *Canto general*, the actor of all the suffering and achievement of *pueblo*, and the narrator who tells a tale that he experiences, but that is not truly his own. On the historical plane of reference the familiar topic of 'América en la historia', which is on its way to becoming a literary convention among Latin American writers, receives a most dramatic treatment

---

[1] Octavio Paz, op. cit., p. 18.
[2] Leopoldo Zea, *El pensamiento latinoamericano* (2 vols., Mexico, 1965), vol. i, p. 33.

that is crucial to the over-all meaning of the *Canto general*. An adequate examination of this type belongs more specifically to the history of ideas, and the literature on this subject is already immense.[1] Arturo Ardao has described this process of using history to define and describe America on all levels of reference:

> Por esa vía América se descubre a sí misma como objeto filosófico. Se descubre en la realidad concreta de su historia y de su cultura, y aún en su naturaleza física en cuanto sostén, contorno y condición de su espiritualidad.... La recapitulación, así, de nuestro pasado espiritual, se convierte en elemento decisivo de nuestro destino como cultura. La historia bien entendida de la filosofía es siempre una vuelta a la tradición filosófica para hacerla participar en la meditación del presente.[2]

Therefore, in describing America and the traditional heroes, Neruda describes himself:

> ... esta historia de América, sus venturas y desventuras, y su viejo dolor recién ahora llorado, no es sino la historia pretérita del poeta referida desde sus orígenes más remotos, desde su comienzo primero. ... Hay una relación sin duda entre aquellos viejos dolores y los suyos

---

[1] The works on this subject are many, but the best general book on the history of ideas is L. Zea, op. cit., especially vol. i, pp. 1-61. See also *Esquema para una historia de las ideas en Iberoamérica* (Filosofía y Letras, Mexico, 1956). This work contains essays on the influence of German historical philosophy on Latin American thought (pp. 61-89), and a very good essay entitled 'Ortega el americano' (pp. 93-120), which discusses the influence of the Spanish philosopher on Latin-American thought. See also 'América en la historia', *Revista de historia de las ideas*, No. 1 (1959), pp. 121-31. For a discussion of the quest for an authentic culture through an examination of the historical past see J. Franco, op. cit., pp. 205-25. Another stimulating book is J. García-Bacca, *Antropología filosófica contemporánea* (Caracas, 1957); this develops the same ideas about the ontological status of America put forward by O'Gorman, op. cit. E. Mayz Vallenilla, *El problema de América* (Caracas, 1959), has an interesting essay 'Examen de nuestra conciencia cultural' (pp. 11-45). He prefaces this work with a poem by Neruda (*Oda al presente*). All these writers stress the importance of understanding and assimilating the historical past, in order to 'explain' the identity of the contemporary Latin-American man. All this is evident in the *Canto general*, and although most of the literature on the subject is to be found in Mexico, it has become a common American topic. See, for example, F. Schwartzmann, op. cit., pp. 63-80, pp. 111 ff. The subject is also treated by A. P. Hogg, op. cit., pp. 102-22, 132, 147 ff., and on p. 517 she concludes: 'far from being a unique case, therefore, the Mexican quest is representative of a search for identity which is common to Latin America as a whole.' Neruda describes the past in order to define and describe himself, and outline a common *americanidad* of all people on the continent.

[2] A. Ardao, 'El historicismo y la filosofía americana', *C.A.*, No. 4 (July-Aug. 1946), pp. 109-18.

THE SOCIAL AND HISTORICAL PLANES 155

actuales, que parecen ser la manifestación presente de aquel dolor acumulado por los siglos.[1]

This relationship is, of course, the structural order of Hombre ⇌ Tierra, which is discernible in the image of the tree, for example. Once again the landscape embodies for Neruda a whole range of meanings on the historical plane. For Neruda, the examination of *pueblo* and the historical past becomes a solution to a personal ontological problem which he incorporates into the collective experience of all people of America both past and present. This question is relevant to this inquiry in so far as the imagery and its structure clearly reflect historical themes. The events of the past are a buried language which can be resurrected out of the earth as a lesson for the present. These events also serve to reinforce the reference of images mobilized in support of an argument in a situation, and, as the last chapter pointed out, the chronology of history in the *Canto general* only serves to demonstrate the continual proof of this argument, which is enshrined in the landscape and its roots in the earth. As a result of this, images such as *tierra*, *oro*, *árbol* contain abiding historical references, which are repeated throughout the *Canto general*, and also serve to identify the poet as actor and narrator in any event described.[2] The importance of language as an image in this respect is evident, for, as with the cries of *pueblo* which are collected together in the voice of each *libertador*, the poet collects each individual story into his own mouth, and thereby the action of unification achieves several meanings. First, it unites the individuals into *pueblo*; second, it identifies the individual experience of the poet with the collective experiences of *pueblo* both past and present; and third,

[1] S. Cabrera, 'Primera teoría del *Canto general*', *Número* (Mar.–June 1951), p. 193. This article (pp. 189–95) is most interesting, as Cabrera is practically the only critic who has taken the view that the social and political themes enlarge the scope of the poetry: ' . . . lo político o social inserto, lejos de molestar a lo poético, le confiere una dimensión especial y una especial resonancia, . . .' (p. 192).

[2] H. A. Murena, 'A propósito del *Canto general* de Pablo Neruda', *Sur*, No. 198 (Apr. 1951), pp. 52–8. Murena sees in the poem an attempt to define man's relationship with his environment, and also the common attempt to define a meaningful past for the Latin American. He points out the historical associations that stones, roots, land, water, etc., acquire throughout the poem, but he is quick to censure Neruda for being negative in his appraisal of the past. Murena thinks that Neruda has condemned all non-American people. For a similar view see Monegal, op. cit., pp. 238–45.

the language of these past events is given a voice, through the poet, to survive into the present.

> Yo vengo a hablar por vuestra boca muerta.
> A través de la tierra juntad todos
> los silenciosos labios derramados
> y desde el fondo habladme toda esta larga noche,
> como si yo estuviera con vosotros anclado,
> contadme todo, cadena a cadena,
> eslabón a eslabón, y paso a paso, . . .
>
> (i. 347–8)

For this reason the structural properties of language lead to its communication properties. Language as a logical structure of parts becomes a living and long-forgotten story told by the poet. This illustrates one of the most important aspects of the historical references in the *Canto general*: that the link with the past is a recollection of the poet's forgotten past. So the personal nature of the experience may be viewed on a more general plane, without losing sight of the fact that it originates in the mind of one individual, the poet. The linking of public and private is also brought out in Neruda's identification of *tierra* with the female form, for it reinforces the idea of going back to the beginning in order to be reborn on a personal and collective level. To answer the question about one's future and present circumstances, the poet has to cure the work of time and go back and find the beginning. As the last chapter demonstrated, the links with the earth are not only productive in a natural sense; they also refer to the origins of man in the earth, continually recovered and re-enacted as a rite.[1] Through

---

[1] i. 394. The death of Valdivia is incorporated into the tree:

> Luego, en el pecho entramos una lanza
> y el corazón alado como un ave
> entregamos al árbol araucano.
> Subió un rumor de sangre hasta su copa.
> Entonces, de la tierra
> hecha de nuestros cuerpos, nació el canto . . .
> Yo hundí los dientes en aquella corola
> cumpliendo el rito de la tierra:
>> 'Dame tu frío, extranjero malvado.
>> Dame tu valor de gran tigre.'

The significance of this 'rite' is that the Spanish conquest and its violence and death are ritualistically incorporated or passed over to the other side (see L.S., op. cit., pp. 32–3), turning death into life, disorder into order, and so on.

THE SOCIAL AND HISTORICAL PLANES 157

the images of *Tierra* and *Océano* the poet is continually able to re-establish contact with the past and re-enact the forgotten events:

> Y así de tierra a tierra fui tocando
> el barro americano, mi estatura,
> y subió por mis venas el olvido
> recostado en el tiempo, hasta que un día
> estremeció mi boca su lenguaje.
>
> (i. 705)

This passage occurs in the final section of the poem entitled *Yo soy* (i. 693–722), where the poet, now that he has described America and the past as a succession of events, feels ready, in this last part of the *Canto general*, to define and describe himself anew in the light of these experiences, as they are contained in one structure, i.e. his own body. In the above passage the earth and the shape of the poet are immediately confused, and the buried and forgotten past rises through the earth and the poet, to emerge out of his mouth as a language which is derived from elswhere. Here, as always, there is a neat set of relationships, for the poet is also a tree with roots in the soil, and the past rises through the tree to acquire a voice through the leaves, which are also compared to *labios*.[1]

When the passage of history is viewed in such a wide perspective, the conflicts of Spaniard *v.* Indian tend to diminish, since they all become part of the common body of the past. Conflict becomes assimilated by time into the sea and the earth, and the names which were *conquistadores* reappear centuries later as the names of *pueblo*. In *Los conquistadores* the Spanish names are enumerated, as they arrive to possess the land:

> Son Arias, Reyes, Rojas, Maldonados,
> hijos del desamparo castellano, . . .
>
> (i. 351)

This is 1519, and picking up the order of events some years later, the poet mentions these names of individuals as they are killed by the Araucanian Indians:

> Ved cómo caen en la tierra
> los hijos ásperos del odio,

[1] i. 320:
Tierra mía sin nombre, sin América,
estambre equinoccial, lanza de púrpura,
tu aroma me trepó por las raíces
hasta la copa que bebía, hasta la más delgada
palabra aún no nacida de mi boca.

> Villagras, Mendozas, Reinosos,
> Reyes, Morales, Alderetes,
> rodaron hacia el fondo blanco
> de las Américas glaciales.
>
> (i. 395–6)

The emphasis in the final lines is less on the conflict and more on the descent of these people back into the earth, where the act of conflict becomes progressively less important when related to the cyclical pattern of life. Several centuries later they will have risen, with the same names, through the *árbol–pueblo* to become parts of the tree:

> Sánchez, Reyes, Ramírez, Núñez, Álvarez.
> Estos nombres son como los cimientos de Chile.
> El pueblo es el cimiento de la patria.
>
> (i. 569)

Names are only particular and visible instances of a larger and invisible pattern which manifests itself in *pueblo* and *patria*. In the same passage the poet continues to identify his 'persona' with the collectivity:

> Yo me llamo como ellos, como los que murieron.
> Yo soy tambien Ramírez, Muñoz, Pérez, Fernández.
> Me llamo Álvarez, Núñez, Tapia, López, Contreras.
>
> (i. 570)

Pueblo, therefore, is made up of all individuals, be they Spanish or Indian, and the movement of history serves as proof in support of this argument.[1]

The ordering properties of history are paramount in the *Canto general*. The poet and the people renew contact with the past in order to understand rather than to blame.[2] The structure which the poet discerns, the abiding growth of *árbol–pueblo*, the continuous rebirth out of the soil through work, only achieves contact with the past in a ritualistic way. But this ritual has a structure that endows the present with purpose and meaning; and, like a rite, it is constantly repeated by the poet and the other participants in order to re-establish and refresh their links with *tierra*, and to order the disorder of life and endow it with a purpose. Because of

---

[1] See Monegal, op. cit., p. 243, for a contrary view.
[2] J. Franco, op. cit., pp. 220–3.

THE SOCIAL AND HISTORICAL PLANES

this the poet ritualistically relives and narrates good and bad events, so that by the action of the rite they can all pass to the winning side and be integrated into a pattern or order of nature[1]

. . . .
mis ojos no vinieron para morder olvido:
mis labios se abren sobre todo el tiempo, y todo el tiempo,
no sólo una parte del tiempo ha gastado mis manos.
Por eso te hablaré de estos dolores que quisiera apartar,
te obligaré a vivir una vez mas entre sus quemaduras,
no para detenernos, como en una estación, al partir,
ni tampoco para golpear con la frente la tierra,
ni para llenarnos el corazón con agua salada,
sino para caminar conociendo, para tocar la rectitud
con decisiones infinitamente cargadas de sentido,
para que la severidad sea una condición de la alegría para
que así seamos invencibles.

(i. 460)

The poet shows the opposed tendencies of history subsumed into an eternal order, which is achieved by marrying all these antagonisms and incoherences into a larger framework. This framework is the imagery and its interconnected references, which point to the over-all themes of the *Canto general*. In this way any event or experience becomes assimilated to a larger structure which holds the *Canto general* together. In the meticulous and exhaustive recollecting of events both individual and collective, private and public, past and present, Neruda incorporates the events of the past into his framework, so that there is a continual relationship between a particular event or experience and a general principle which is dominant throughout the poem. This results in a series of images that are continually repeated throughout, and which come together to form a set of interlocking relationships that are the guiding principles of any event in the *Canto general*. Instead of looking for a beginning, middle, and end, we should view the *Canto general* as in some ways a loose architectural complex, which could have parts added to or subtracted from the structure without destroying the over-all organic unity. The whole structure of the *Canto general* can be discerned in each of its parts, and it is this characteristic that this chapter has tried to illustrate.

[1] L.S., op. cit., pp. 32–3.

CONCLUSION

Qué era el hombre? En qué parte de su conversación abierta entre los almacenes y los silbidos, en cuál de sus movimientos metálicos vivía lo indestructible, lo imperecedero, la vida? (i. 337)

THE most noticeable feature of Neruda's imagery in the *Canto general* is the notion of order. The poet's admiration of the walls at Machu-Picchu is carried right through to his exaltation of *pueblo* as an ordered and enduring system that reflects the order and harmony of nature. For this reason he is able to celebrate every object that he sees or touches in terms of its internal structure, which reflects the larger external structure of the universe. This is the most significant fact to emerge from our study of the *Canto general*, and provides the key to an understanding not only of this poem, but also of his later work, for example the *Odas elementales*.

The notion of order and disorder can be seen in Neruda's organization of the major images in the poem, especially in the contrast between images of land and sea, frequently mingled in a formal manner, with recurring oppositions of *ola* and *cordillera*, and other instances featuring *espuma* and *nieve*. This is particularly true when the poet describes Chile, with the juxtaposition of waves and mountains. But this contrast between land and sea operates throughout the whole of the *Canto general* in differing transformations of life and death, sound and silence, light and dark, *pueblo* and oligarchy. Neruda may be said to combine these images in three ways, which are recurring features of this technique throughout the poem.

Firstly, he confuses images of land invaded by sea to convey themes of social disorder, moral confusion, and death. Secondly, he borrows land attributes to form sea attributes (*pétalo de mar*). This is common when referring to *patria* or *pueblo* as a whole to exemplify their universality and endurance. The third way in which Neruda combines images is by far the most common and the most important in the whole poem. He refers to one image in terms of another, using an instrumental set related sometimes to land, sometimes to sea: different images are referred to in terms of each other, but in an ordered manner. A good example of this

CONCLUSION

would be his frequent mingling of parts of a wall with parts of a rose, as in *pétalos de piedra* (i. 341). Another example, a development of the second type, would be the mingling of wave and rose (i. 670). In the gold-mining sequence he does this with *árbol* and *mineral* (i. 613), and in the whole of the Machu-Picchu sequence (i. 335–48) images of land and sea are continually compared and contrasted to exemplify the survival of the city and to denote its central place in Neruda's universe, uniting both land and sea:

> Madre de piedra, espuma de los cóndores.
> Alto arrecife de la aurora humana.   (i. 339)

The persistent exchange of attributes in the three ways described is the fundamental technique of the imagery of the *Canto general*.[1]

This combination of images in repeated oppositions is both a fixed poetic language in the *Canto general* and the abiding speech of Neruda's later poetry. The separate images (*ola, rosa, piedra, árbol, nieve, espuma, raíz*, to name a few), with their attributes and fields of association, are combined with a consistency that implies a set of formulaic devices. The pairing of different images, such as *árbol* and *ola*, points to further enormously intricate fields of reference which persist in Neruda's later poetry. *Oda a las aves de Chile* (i. 1026–31) is wholly structured in terms of this exchange of land and sea attributes, which enrich one another through constant repetition. Another example, in *Cien sonetos de amor* (ii. 193), exchanges attributes between *rosa–ola, árbol–ola, ola–piedra*, and *pétalo–piedra*, all constant fields of comparison in the *Canto general*. This example illustrates the second and third types of linking images mentioned above. Here, the wave-cycle and the tree-cycle are formally apostrophized in the exchange of attributes:

> Oh radiante magnolia desatada en la espuma,
> magnética viajera cuya muerte florece
> y eternamente vuelve a ser y a no ser nada:
> sal rota, deslumbrante movimiento marino.   (ii. 293)

---

[1] This tendency in Calderón's imagery is noted in E. M. Wilson's pioneer study 'The four elements in the dramatic imagery of Calderón', *Modern Language Review*, xxxi (1936), pp. 34–47. Another article where image structure points the way to structure of thought is Angel L. Cilvetti, 'Silogismo, correlación e imagen poética en el teatro de Calderón', *Romanische Forschungen*, 80 (1968), pp. 459–97. Cilvetti shows how correlative and parallel patterns of imagery can be linked to the syllogistic mode of argument. In our case the argument in Neruda's poetry is reflected in the formal opposition and exchange of major images and their associative fields, such as *Océano* and *Tierra*.

CONCLUSION

This technique of exchanging attributes reflects Neruda's concern for order and system in both the organization of the imagery and the themes that the poetry embodies.[1]

The poet's search for order and coherence is reflected also in the language of the poem; but it is a language of stone, mineral, and earth. Languages have simple structures, which make do with numerous elements. The opposition between the simplicity of these structures and the multiplicity of elements (or possible sounds) is expressed by the fact that several elements compete to occupy the same positions in one structure. In the *Canto general* the images become the constituent parts of that language sought so eagerly by the poet, for '. . . language can be said to be a condition of culture because the material out of which language is built is of the same type out of which the whole culture is built: logical relations, oppositions, correlations, and the like.'[2] Neruda himself echoes this in his definition of *patria*, and in his insistence on the discovery of a language to express the order of a society. The language of the *Canto general* becomes inseparable from the cultural framework that gives rise to it, and the poet's search for order brings together the two poles of Neruda's experience: nature and language. The word and the stone are united in the poem's imagery where previously they tended to exist apart, or, as Neruda expresses it, *una permanencia de piedra y de palabra* (i. 341). In his earlier poetry Neruda observed a world of signs which he could not comprehend. In *Unidad* (i. 177) the constituent parts have not come together into the language for which the poet is searching. All these forms are defined as *confusas unidades*. Looking back with hindsight, it is understandable that the earlier poems of *Residencia en la tierra* should appear as examples of a search for a language only partially understood and not fully comprehended. Nevertheless, there is an increasing enthusiasm and approximation towards that language, tentatively formulated in *España en el corazón*, and triumphantly realized in the *Canto general*.

[1] Neruda does not develop the medieval world-picture of four elements as Calderón does (Wilson, op. cit.). He does consciously exploit land and sea images, and confuse them for his purposes. Neruda uses what Wilson would call the 'visual exchange of elements' in his *nieve–espuma* references (Wilson, 37–40). But Neruda tends to combine different images (which can all be reduced to land and sea) quite freely: e.g. *piedra–árbol*, *raíz–oro*. This might be ascribed to Wilson's 'horses, birds, and boats' category, where different images are referred to in terms of each other: e.g., *rosa de piedra* or *pétalo de mar* (Wilson, 40–1).

[2] L.S., 'Linguistics and anthropology', *Structural Anthropology*, pp. 68–9.

A further example of the notion of order which is so important in the *Canto general* is the scale of the poem. The values underlying the language are measured in human terms, and the concepts of history and the permanence of social forms are all weighed by the human scale. In many cases the body of the poet becomes the recipient of *pueblo* or *patria*. The imagery in the poem shows how the body, with its multiple possibilities as a device for poetic comparison, becomes the universal criterion. The body and its organization is for Neruda the highest principle of order in nature. This persists in the *Memorial de Isla Negra*, published fourteen years later. In this autobiographical poem Neruda continues his definition and description of man in himself, but on a much more intimate level. Since the *Canto general* he has mapped out the boundaries of his own universe, within which he confidently moves. The details of this world have deep implications in the *Canto general* as well as in later work.

Neruda has come close to defining an ideal state of man within a natural setting in the *Canto general*. He has also deepened his understanding of man and nature and the forces of renewal which lie within human powers. Although this is shown in the broader frame of reference acquired by the imagery, it also points to a quest for an ordered or harmonious social existence.

The rain forests of Southern Chile and the coast of Isla Negra, where waves are continually locked in combat, are not so much geographically precise spots to be pinpointed as nature ordered through poetry. They are examples of a *locus amoenus* where man and nature exist in harmony. In the poem Neruda gains access to this ideal state at different points in time, and the struggle is to strive continually and recover what is lost. The collective existence where man enjoys the fruits of nature *in commune* is an inheritance of values achieved through work and collective effort. Neruda's poetry has achieved echoes of history and culture through the far-reaching powers of association possessed by his imagery.

In the Golden Age, as described in the Renaissance, the ideal state of man was destroyed by the pursuit of wealth, namely of precious metals such as gold and silver. In the *Canto general* Neruda uses old tropes to suit new historical facts, giving them a Marxian gloss. Worker and gold exist in a society corrupted by commercial exploitation: but the ideal state is destroyed because the gold does not remain in the hands of the people, whereas formerly it was because the gold did not remain in the earth.[1] The work of *pueblo* is another example of Neruda's search for order. The gold-mining sequence contrasts the work of *hombre* with the movement and cycle of the land (*árbol–rosa*) and the sea (*ola*). Man's origins in nature become quiet allusions in Neruda's later poetry. In the *Odas elementales* he continues the attempt to outline an ordered existence. For this reason a poem such as *Oda al cobre* (i. 1037–42) gains in meaning not only because of the formal exchange of attributes between *hombre–mineral* and *árbol–mineral* uncovered in the *Canto general*, but also because the poet has built up a network of references to previous occurrences in other contexts. The poem looks back to the copper-mining sequences in the *Canto general*, and so Neruda refers back and imitates himself. Self-quotation becomes a new area of growth and enrichment in his poetry. The tendency to self-imitation makes the *Canto general* a watershed in the development of his poetry; it synthesizes much of the previous work, and clarifies abiding associations between major images which Neruda had not fully worked out in his earlier poetry. Finally, the *Canto general* provides him with a set of themes that he never abandons, especially the social, historical, and political phenomena set down in the poem. These themes enter the poet's ritual of experienced detail, and even when Neruda is writing at a personal level, he implies these more public and impersonal areas of meaning.[2] The reason why he refuses to forgo these themes is that Neruda has always sought to discover in his poetry the nature of man: to do this, he has had to find his way back to an understanding of how man is related to nature.

[1] H. Levin, *The Myth of the Golden Age in the Renaissance* (London, 1970), p. 23.
[2] For a view of Neruda's recent poetry which sees Neruda as trying to recapture a lost ideal, a vanished innocence, with emphasis on *lo perdido*, see Ben Belitt's excellent Foreword in *Pablo Neruda: a New Decade (Poems, 1958–1967)* (New York, 1969), xxxiv–xxxv, xli.

BIBLIOGRAPHY OF WORKS CITED

A. WORKS BY PABLO NERUDA

Obras completas, 3rd edn. (2 vols., Losada, Buenos Aires, 1968).
Poesías completas (Losada, Buenos Aires, 1951).
Obras completas, 2nd edn. (Losada, Buenos Aires, 1962).
Obra poética, ed. Juvencio Valle (10 vols., Cruz del Sur, Santiago, 1947–8).
Selección, ed. Arturo Aldunate Phillips (Nascimiento, Santiago, 1943).
Viajes (Nascimiento, Santiago, 1955).
'Las vidas del poeta. Memorias y recuerdos de Pablo Neruda', 10 parts, *O Cruzeiro Internacional* (Rio de Janeiro, 16 Jan.–1 July 1962).
Las piedras de Chile (Losada, Buenos Aires, 1960). With photographs by Antonio Quintana.
Una casa en la arena (ed. Lumen, Barcelona, 1966). With photographs by Sergio Larraín.
Discursos (with Nicanor Parra. Nascimiento, Santiago, 1962).
'Sobre una poesía sin pureza', *Caballo verde para la poesía*, No. 1 (Madrid, Oct. 1935). Also found in *Obras completas*, 3rd edn. ii. 1040–1, and *Obra poética*, vol. 7, pp. 49–51.
'Los frescos de Xavier Guerrero en Chillán', *Ars*, vol. 1, No. 5 (Mexico, May 1943), pp. 60–2. Only the Introduction to the article is by Neruda.
'Visiones de las hijas de Albión y el viajero mental, de William Blake', trans. Neruda, *Cruz y Raya*, No. 20 (Madrid, Nov. 1934), pp. 85–109.
'Cartas y sonetos de la muerte de Quevedo', *Cruz y Raya*, No. 33 (Madrid, Dec. 1935), pp. 83–101.

B. CRITICAL WORKS ON NERUDA

AGUIRRE, M. *Genio y figura de Pablo Neruda*, 2nd edn. (Ed. Universitaria, Buenos Aires, 1967).
ALAZRAKI, J. *Poética y poesía de Pablo Neruda* (Las Americas Publishing Co., New York, 1965).
ALONSO, A. *Poesía y estilo de Pablo Neruda*, 3rd. edn. (Ed. Sudamericana, Buenos Aires, 1966).
BELITT, B. *Selected Poems of Pablo Neruda* (Grove Press, New York, 1961), Translator's Foreword, pp. 30–8.
—— 'Pablo Neruda and the "gigantesque"', *Poetry*, vol. 80, No. 2 (May 1952), pp. 116–18.
—— *Pablo Neruda: a New Decade* (*Poems, 1958–1967*) (Grove Press, New York, 1969).

BELITT, B. 'The mourning Neruda', *Mundus Artium*, vol. 1, No. 1 (Winter 1967), pp. 14–23.
—— 'Poems from the *Canto general*', *Poetry*, vol. 79, No. 4 (Jan. 1952), pp. 204–11.
BELLINI, G. *Introduzione a Neruda* (La Goliardica, Milan, 1966).
CABRERA, S. 'Primera teoría del *Canto general*', *Número* (Montevideo, Mar.–June 1951), pp. 189–95.
CARDONA PEÑA, A. 'Pablo Neruda: Breve historia de sus libros', *C.A.* No. 6 (Mexico, Nov.–Dec. 1950), pp. 257–89.
—— *Pablo Neruda y otros ensayos* (Ed. de Andrea, Mexico, 1955), pp. 7–84.
ESCUDERO, A. M. 'Fuentes para el conocimiento de Neruda', *Mapocho*, ii, No. 3 (1964), pp. 249–79. An excellent bibliography of all material about Neruda. Now also in ii. 1503–98.
LOYOLA, H. 'Los modos de autoreferencia en la obra de Pablo Neruda', Ed. de *Aurora*, 2a época No. 3–4 (Santiago, 1964).
—— *Ser y morir en Pablo Neruda* (Ed. Santiago, 1967).
MARCENAC, J. *Pablo Neruda* (Ed. Seghers, Paris, 1963).
MELÉNDEZ, C. 'Pablo Neruda en su extremo imperio', *R.H.M.*, No. 1, (Oct. 1936), pp. 1–32.
MONGUIÓ, L. *Selected Poems of Pablo Neruda* (Grove Press, New York, 1961), Introduction, pp. 7–29.
MURENA, H. 'A propósito del *Canto general* de Pablo Neruda', *Sur*, No. 198 (Buenos Aires, Apr. 1951), pp. 52–8.
POLT, J. H. R. 'Elementos gongorinos en *"El gran océano"* de Pablo Neruda', *R.H.M.* xxvii (1961), pp. 25–31.
PRING-MILL, R. *The Heights of Macchu Picchu*, trans. N. Tarn (Jonathan Cape, London, 1966), Preface, pp. 7–13.
PUCCINI, D. 'Lettura del *Canto general*', *Società*, No. 4 (Turin, Dec. 1950), pp. 585–619.
RIVERO DE LA CALLE, M. 'Pablo Neruda, poeta y naturalista', *Islas*, vol. 3, No. 3 (Cuba, May–Aug. 1961), pp. 99–106.
RODRÍGUEZ MONEGAL, E. *El viajero inmóvil: Introducción a Pablo Neruda* (Losada, Buenos Aires, 1966).
SILVA CASTRO, R. *Pablo Neruda* (Ed. Universitaria, Santiago, 1964).
VALBUENA BRIONES, A. 'La aventura poética de Pablo Neruda', *C.A.* xx (1961), pp. 205–23. This article was incorporated into *Literatura hispanoamericana* (Ed. Gustavo Gili, Barcelona, 1962), pp. 432–51. This is vol. 4 of *Historia de la literatura española*, by A. Valbuena Prat.

C. OTHER WORKS

ACOSTA, J. *Historia natural y moral de las Indias* [1591], ed. E. O'Gorman (F.C.E., Mexico, 1962).
ALONSO, D. *Seis calas en la expresión literaria española* (with Carlos Bousoño), 3rd edn., aumentada (Ed. Gredos, Madrid, 1963).
ARDAO, A. 'El historicismo y la filosofía americana', *C.A.* No. 4 (July–Aug. 1946), pp. 109–18.

BARROS-ARANA, D. *Compendio de la historia de América* (4 pts., Santiago, 1865).
BINGHAM, H. *Lost City of the Incas—the story of Macchu Picchu and its Builders* (Phoenix House Ltd., London, 1951).
—— *Machu Picchu, a Citadel of the Incas, Report of the Explorations and Excavations in 1911, 1912, and 1915* (O.U.P., London, 1930).
BLAKE, W. *Complete Writings*, ed. Geoffrey Keynes (O.U.P., London, 1966).
CARRERA ANDRADE, J. 'The new American and his point of view towards poetry', *Poetry*, vol. 62, No. 2 (May 1943), pp. 88–104.
CILVETTI, A. L. 'Silogismo, correlación e imagen poética en el teatro de Calderón', *Romanische Forschungen*, 80 (1968), pp. 459–97.
CURTIUS, E. R. *European Literature and the Latin Middle Ages* (Bollingen Series, New York, 1953).
ELIADE, M. *The Myth of the Eternal Return* (Bollingen Series, London, 1965).
—— *Myth and Reality* (Allen and Unwin, London, 1964).
ERDMAN, G. E., JR., 'Arboreal figures in the Golden Age sonnet', *P.M.L.A.*, vol. 84 (1969), pp. 587–95.
FRANCO, J. *The Modern Culture of Latin America: Society and the Artist* (Pall Mall Press, London, 1967).
GARCÍA-BACCA, J. *Antropología filosófica contemporánea* (Universidad Central de Venezuela, Caracas, 1957).
GOODALL, J. D. *Las aves de Chile* (with A. W. Johnson and B. Philippi) (2 vols., Platt, establecimientos Gráficos, Buenos Aires, 1946–51).
GREEN, O. H. *Spain and the Western Tradition* (4 vols., University of Wisconsin Press, Wisconsin, 1963–6).
HERRING, H. *A History of Latin America* (Jonathan Cape, London, 1955).
HEYERDAHL, T. *American Indians in the Pacific* (Allen and Unwin, London, 1952).
HOGG, A. P. 'The search for identity in post-revolutionary Mexican writing', unpublished thesis (London, 1967).
HUDSON, W. H. *Birds of La Plata*, with plates by H. Gronwold (2 vols., London, 1920).
JONES, R. O. 'The poetic unity of the *Soledades* of Góngora', *B.H.S.* xxxi (1954), pp. 189–204.
KUBLER, G. 'Machu Picchu', *Perspecta, Y.A.J.* vi, (New Haven, Conn., 1960), pp. 48–55.
LEACH, E. [Ed.] *The Structural Study of Myth and Totemism* (Tavistock Publications, London, 1967).
LÉVI-STRAUSS, C. *Totemism*, trans. Rodney Needham (Merlin Press, London, 1964).
—— *The Savage Mind* (Weidenfeld and Nicolson, London, 1966).
—— *Structural Anthropology*, trans. Claire Jacobson and Brooke Grundfest Schoepf (Basic Books, New York, 1963).
—— 'Les chats de Charles Baudelaire', *L'Homme* (Jan.–Apr. 1962), pp. 5–21.
LEVIN, H. *The Myth of the Golden Age in the Renaissance* (Faber and Faber, London, 1970).

MAYZ VALLENILLA, E. *El problema de América* (Publicaciones de la Dirección de Cultura de la Universidad Central, Caracas, 1959).
MEANS, P. A. 'The rebellion of Tupac Amaru II (1780–81)', *H.A.H.R.* ii (Feb. 1919), pp. 1–25.
MORLEY, S. G. *The Ancient Maya*. 3rd edn., revised by G. W. Brainerd (Stanford U.P., Stanford, 1956).
NICHOLSON, I. *Mexican and Central American Mythology* (Paul Hamlyn, London, 1967).
O'GORMAN, E. *The Invention of america: an Inquiry into the Historical Nature of the New World and the Meaning of its History* (Indiana University Press, Bloomington, 1961).
PAZ, O. *El laberinto de la soledad*, 4th edn. (F.C.E., Mexico, 1964).
PELLICER, C. *Material poético, 1918–1961* (Universidad Nacional Autónoma de México, Mexico, 1962).
QUEVEDO, F. DE. *Antología poética*, 3rd edn. (Losada, Buenos Aires, 1952).
SAPIR, E. *Culture, Language and Personality: Selected Essays* (University of California Press, Berkeley, 1966).
SCHWARTZMANN, F. *El sentimiento de lo humano en América* (Ed. Universitaria, Santiago, 1950).
SPITZER, L. *La enumeración caótica en la poesía moderna: Colección de estudios estilísticos* (Instituto de Filología, Buenos Aires, 1945).
THOMSON, G. *Marxism and Poetry* (International Publishers, New York, 1946).
VAILLANT, G. C. *Aztecs of Mexico* (Pelican Books, London, 1965).
WESTHEIM, P. *The Art of Ancient Mexico* (Doubleday and Co., New York, 1965).
WILSON, E. M. 'The four elements in the dramatic imagery of Calderón', *Modern Language Review*, xxxi (1936), pp. 34–47.
ZEA, L. *El pensamiento latinoamericano* (2 vols., Ed. Pomarca, Mexico, 1965).
—— 'América en la historia', *Revista de Historia de Ideas*, No. 1 (1959), pp. 121–31.
—— *Esquema para una historia de las ideas en Iberoamérica* (Universidad Nacional Autónoma de México, Mexico, 1956).

D. DICTIONARIES

Diccionario de la lengua española, 18th edn. (Real Academia Española, Madrid, 1956).
SANTAMARÍA, F. J. *Diccionario general de americanismos* (3 vols., Ed. Pedro Robredo, Mexico, 1942).

INDEX

Acosta, J., 74 n.
Aguirre, M., 87 n., 103 n., 114 n.
Alonso, A., 55 n., 85 n.
Alonso, D., 2 n.
Araucana, La, 52
Araucanians, 51, 86, 87, 88, 89 f., 135, 136 n., 157
Ardao, A., 154
Argentina, 122, 124, 148 n.
Atl, Dr., 95 n.
Aztec(s), 69, 71, 79, 81, 82, 86, 87, 120 n., 124

Barros Arana, D., 87 n.
Baudelaire, C., xv n.
Belitt, B., xiv, 164
Bellini, G., xvi n.
Bingham, H., 3 n.
Blake, W., xvii, 83 n.
Bolívar, S., 106, 111 n.
Bousoño, C., 2 n.

Cabrera, S., 155 n.
Calderón, P., 53 n., 161 n., 162 n.
Canto General, sections discussed:
  La Lámpara en la tierra, 2, 4, 6, 33, 66, 68, 72, 74, 75, 81, 82, 83, 86, 94, 135, 136
  Alturas de Macchu-Picchu, 2, 4, 5, 13, 17, 22, 23, 24, 31, 32, 33, 43, 45, 47, 60, 62 n., 81, 82, 94, 112 n., 114 n., 138, 142
  Los conquistadores, 23, 24, 88, 94, 114, 157
  Los libertadores, 8, 24, 27, 58, 102, 107, 113, 136
  La arena traicionada, 118
  Canto general de Chile, 28, 46
  La tierra se llama Juan, 134 n.
  Las flores de Punitaqui, 29, 31, 33, 68, 125, 141
  El gran océano, 6, 7, 18, 33, 58, 63 n., 72, 73
  Yo soy, 157
Cardona Peña, A., xvi n.
Carrera Andrade, J., xiv n.
Caupolicán, 140, 143 n.
Chillán, xvi n.

Cilvetti, A., 161 n.
Cuauhtémoc, 117 n., 139
Curtius, E., 2 n.

Eliade, M., xvii n., 129 n.
Ercilla, A. de, 73
Erdman, G. Jr., 149 n.

Franco, J., xiii n., 154 n., 158 n.

García-Bacca, J., 154 n.
Golden Age, 79–80, 82 n., 84, 97 n., 149 n., 163
Góngora, L., 53 n., 82 n., 97 n.
Goodall, J., 87 n.
Green, O., 79 n.
Guerrero, X., xvi n.

Herring, H., 80 n.
Heyerdahl, T., 76 n., 82 n.
Hogg, A., 83 n., 117 n., 154 n.
Hudson, W., 87 n.

Imagery: Main images of the *Canto General*:
  árbol, 8–11, 13 n., 24, 26, 27 n., 60 n., 86, 88, 90, 92, 95, 97–9, 102–3, 113, 117, 131, 133, 135–52, 155, 158, 161, 162 n., 164
  copa, 8, 57–8, 76, 103 n., 113, 148, 149–50
  flor (rosa, pétalo), 11, 15, 16, 31, 48–9, 60 n., 141, 141 n., 142, 151, 151 n., 160–2, 164
  océano, 6–8, 10, 11, 18, 20, 22–4, 26, 29, 33–5, 50, 53, 60, 62, 65, 72, 76, 78, 157, 161 n.
  ola, 8, 10–12, 14, 59, 60, 141, 151, 160–1, 164
  oro, 30–2, 35, 79, 91, 97, 125–34, 136, 155, 162 n.
  patria, 2, 8, 17, 19, 46–9, 50–2, 54, 84 n., 85, 89 f., 105, 106 f., 160, 162, 163 n.
  pueblo, 1, 8, 9, 15, 17, 19, 20, 25, 27, 28 n., 30, 34, 46, 49, 50, 51, 53, 58, 67, 70, 82, 84, 85, 94–6, 98, 105, 106 f., 160, 163 n., 164

Imagery (cont.):
   raíz, 20, 91, 92, 97, 99, 139, 140, 148, 161, 162 *n*.
   tierra, passim
Inca, 79, 82, 87, 139

Johnson, A., 87 *n*.
Jones, R., 82 *n*.

Keynes, G., 83 *n*.
Kubler, G., 3 *n*.

Lautaro, 117 *n*., 139, 143 *n*.
Lévi-Strauss, C., xv, xvi, 7 *n*., 28 *n*., 36 *n*., 68 *n*., 84 *n*., 124 *n*., 156 *n*., 159 *n*., 162 *n*.
Levin, H., 164
Linnaeus, 28
L'Ouverture, Toussaint, 117 *n*.
Loyola, H., 31 *n*., 43 *n*., 55 *n*., 65 *n*.

Marcenac, J., 86 *n*.
Martí, J., 106, 143 *n*.
Marxist criticism, 124, 125, 163
Maya(s), 80, 82, 87, 135
Mayz Vallenilla, E., 154 *n*.
Means, P., 112 *n*.
Meléndez, C., 95 *n*., 144 *n*.
Mexico, xvi, 44, 83 *n*., 87, 90, 117 *n*., 118 *n*., 120 *n*., 152, 153, 154 *n*.
Monguió, L., xiv, xv *n*., xvii, 106 *n*., 116 *n*.
Morley, S., 80 *n*.
Murena, H., 155 *n*.

Neruda, P., *other works*:
   'Cartas y sonetos de la muerte de Quevedo', xvii
   casa en la arena, Una, 63 *n*.
   Cien sonetos de amor, 161
   copa de sangre, La, 103 *n*.
   Discursos, xv, 73 *n*., 104 *n*., 106 *n*.
   España en el corazón, 128 *n*., 162
   furias y las penas, Las, 128 *n*.
   Infancia y poesía, 100 *n*.
   Memorial de Isla Negra, 163
   Odas elementales, 16 *n*., 160, 164
   piedras de Chile, Las, 61 *n*.
   Residencia en la tierra, 54, 58 *n*., 75 *n*., 93, 162
   'Sobre una poesía sin pureza', 61 *n*.
   Tercera residencia, 111 *n*.
   'Viaje al corazón de Quevedo', xvii

   Viajes, 56 *n*., 80 *n*.
   'vidas del poeta, Las', 77 *n*., 91 *n*.
   'Visions of the Daughters of Albion and the Mental Traveller by William Blake', xvii
Nicholson, I., 120 *n*.

O'Gorman, E., 74 *n*., 154 *n*.
O'Higgins, B., 117 *n*., 139
Ortega y Gasset, J., 154 *n*.

Parra, N., xv *n*.
Paz, O., xiii, 117 *n*., 118 *n*., 152, 153
Pellicer, C., xiii, xiv
Philippi, R., 87 *n*.
Polt, J., 59 *n*., 60, 75 *n*., 81 *n*., 97 *n*.
Pring-Mill, R., 14 *n*., 15 *n*.
Puccini, D., 134 *n*.

Quetzalcoatl, 120 *n*.
Quevedo, F. de, xvii, 55, 58 *n*., 97 *n*.

Recabarren, E., 106, 107, 109, 110, 111, 116 *n*., 121, 124, 130, 134
Rivera, D., xiii
Rivero de la Calle, M., 105 *n*.
Rodríguez Monegal, E., xiv, 33 *n*., 84 *n*., 103 *n*., 107, 116, 117, 118 *n*., 155 *n*., 158 *n*.
Rosas, J., 122, 123

San Martín, J., 27, 28 *n*., 106, 111, 117 *n*., 143 *n*.
Santamaría, F., 148 *n*.
Sapir, E., 45 *n*.
Schwartzmann, F., 46 *n*., 50 *n*., 154 *n*.
Silva Castro, R., 63 *n*., 65 *n*., 78 *n*., 139 *n*.
Spitzer, L., 2 *n*.

Tarn, N., 14 *n*.
Thomson, G., 125 *n*., 128 *n*., 132 *n*., 133 *n*.
Tupac Amaru, 112, 113, 114, 124, 134, 140, 143 *n*.

Vaillant, G., 71 *n*., 80 *n*., 120 *n*.
Valbuena Briones, A., xvi *n*.
Valdivia, P. de, 143 *n*., 144 *n*., 156 *n*.

Westheim, P., 120 *n*.
Wilson, E., 161 *n*., 162 *n*.

Zea, L., 153, 154 *n*.